The Two Worlds of Tina

The Two Worlds of Tina

Natalee S. Greenfield, Ph.D.

VANTAGE PRESS
New York

While based on extensive professional research and a true clinical story, the names appearing herein have been changed to protect the confidentiality of the subject matter. Any similarity between the names and characters in this book and any real persons, living or dead, is purely coincidental.

FIRST EDITION

All rights reserved, including the right of reproduction in whole or in part in any form.

Copyright © 2006 by Natalee S. Greenfield, Ph.D.

Published by Vantage Press, Inc.
419 Park Ave. South, New York, NY 10016

Manufactured in the United States of America
ISBN: 0-533-15198-8

Library of Congress Catalog Card No.: 2005902102

0 9 8 7 6 5 4 3 2 1

To my husband, Raymond, who has been my love and companion for over sixty years

and

To our daughter, Lynn, and my parents, Corinne and Nathan, whose loving memories will dwell in my heart forever

Contents

Acknowledgments ix
Introduction xi

1. The Nightmare Begins 1
2. A Birthday Wish 10
3. In Search of Home 16
4. Rejected and Abused 25
5. The Spiritual Search 32
6. Eunuchs and Geishas 40
7. A Hero's Welcome 51
8. Let Me Out 59
9. Exposed 67
10. Bigot's Trap 77
11. Who Am I? 84
12. To Kill the Urge 89
13. A Family Man 97
14. Pills for Change 108
15. Becoming One 120
16. You've Got to Help Me 126
17. Conversion Rebirth 136
18. Journey to Freedom 145
19. Farewell Procrustean Bed 156
20. Tina: An American Transsexual 169

Acknowledgments

With gratitude to my husband, Dr. Raymond, for his editorial contributions and ongoing support, and to Larry Kalmbach for his endless enthusiasm and assistance in preparing the book.

I also want to express my deep appreciation to "Tina" and my other patients, who have been a constant source of inspiration to me for half a century in my practice of psychotherapy.

And last but not least, I want to express my deep appreciation and admiration to the pioneers of the scientific community in psychology and related fields who worked toward establishing a quality of life for all individuals.

Introduction

The Two Worlds of Tina is the true story of a transsexual: a biographical journey that recounts the central character's life-long struggle with sexual identity. It was this author's long-term association with her patient that provided an abundance of material, which in turn offered a rich account and rare view of the complex events and relationships that shaped Tina's destiny.

Tina asked me to write a book explaining her plight and those of others who like her are trapped in the Transsexual Phenomena. She wanted to share her story of being a despondent, desperate person who was alienated and tormented by both family and society because of a gender identity problem—a problem that could have been caused by a developmental mishap while still in her mother's womb.

This book is being published twenty-seven years after I first saw Tina as a patient. I have given her a fictitious name, Tina Turner, to protect her, and have also changed the names of others to avoid identifying those closely involved in her life.

The diagnostic criterion for being a transsexual is feeling an intolerable discomfort about one's body, to the point of wanting to rid oneself of one's genitals and to live as a member of the opposite sex. Like transsexuals, transvestites also cross-dress, but do not want to be rid of their genitals. Cross-dressing relieves them of their tension, frustration, and gender discomfort. However, it is not usually done for sexual excitement. The effeminate homosexual might also have characteristics of the opposite sex, but no desire to change his or her anatomical sex or to cross-dress. Homosexuality is no longer classified as a mental disorder, unless it causes the individual persistent distress, which is referred to as being ego-dystonic. These problems can occur in both males and females.

There have been and continue to be scientific advances and discoveries that help explain sexual anomalies. These include: new findings about chromosomes and genes; fetal hormonal sex; hypothalamic sex influence on the fetus; and the role of hormones on the fetus. Scientists have reported that an embryo's human tissue is female during the early weeks of gestation. There can also be a deviation of a hypothalamic malfunction and other chemical mishaps. As a consequence, the anatomy of the fetus might become male while the fetus's brain remains forever female, trapped in a male body. Could this theory explain why there are so many more male transsexuals, transvestites, and homosexuals than female? This mishap could have happened to anyone.

For me, writing this book is more than a clinical psychologist's case history about a patient. When I first met Tina in my office, I was appearing on radio and TV shows regarding another book I wrote, *"First Do No Harm..."* to warn the public about the potential medical hazards of hormones, especially estrogen. Estrogen is used in birth control pills and hormone replacement therapy for women, given to men to treat prostate cancer, and given to transsexuals, often resulting in medical tragedies. I continue to use my pen name, Natalee S. Greenfield, to comply with a court order.

Last but not least, I wanted to write about a major problem that exists in our society. By and large, society still maintains the position that a person should conform to society's Procrustean Bed. In reading Tina's story it will be apparent that all individuals are not created equal, and that the pursuit of life, liberty, and contentment should exist for all regardless of their gender identity. The following paragraphs relate a tale from ancient Greek mythology that I believe illustrates my point.

There is a tale in classical Greek mythology about a robber named Procrustes who lived near Eleusis in Attica. He would kidnap travelers and place them on an iron bed in his abode. To make them conform to the length of the iron bed, he would either amputate their limbs, if they were too long, or stretch the limbs of those he captured if they were too short.

This hypothetical theory of human behavior should be formulated to meet the uniqueness of the individual's needs rather than to tailor the person to fit society's Procrustean Bed. How we may better understand the transsexual and help society to accept the transsexual's inalienable rights to be a contributing member of society is presented in the biography that follows.

1

The Nightmare Begins

Timmy Turner's nightmare began at summer's end in 1937, when he was four years old.

Three or four hours had passed since Timmy had been taken from his mother, and he was soaked with perspiration. The blazing Mississippi sun had turned his father's car into an oven.

Timothy Turner, Sr. drove, sweat dripping from his chin. Big and tall, with construction worker's muscles, he had a lust for women and gambling that was fully developed. When drunk, which was often, he became belligerent and violent. He was separated from his wife, Janet, and lived with someone named Cassandra.

Timmy was terrified of his father and cried, "I want to go home to Mamma."

"Shut up! You wake up your brother, and you'll really have something to cry about."

Timmy's brown eyes were brimming with tears, and nervously he began fingering his sweat-soaked brown curls. To avoid his father's glare, Timmy turned to look at his brother, Joey, who was lying on the back seat.

Timmy was a year older than Joey, but people thought they were twins. Joey was the same height as Timmy and more robust. In contrast, Timmy had a delicate, almost frail, body that gave him a pretty-boy look, like that of a little girl.

Timmy's father slowed the car to read a small handmade

sign nailed to a tree. "Sand Hill!" he said and turned onto a narrow dirt road that led into a heavily wooded area filled with strange sounds and foul smells. The dark, dense woods frightened Timmy so much that he couldn't cry and felt breathless. After a short distance, the forest thinned, and they soon came to a clearing where Timmy could see a log cabin with a front porch.

Timmy's father stopped the car and got out. At the same time, a short, stout woman came down the cabin steps to greet him. She wore an apron over a long-sleeved black dress. Her head was partly covered with a white bonnet. Her gray-white hair was drawn tightly into a bun. Her wrinkled skin was dark and weathered.

Timmy crouched against the back of the car seat. To Timmy she looked like the witch in Hansel and Gretel!

Timmy's father opened the car door and yanked him out. "This here is Jessie. She's Cassandra's half-sister. You and Joey are going to stay with her. She wants you to call her Granny."

Shyly, Timmy looked at the woman, and then tugged at his father's trouser leg, "Please, I want to go home to Mamma!"

"You're staying here." Then Timmy's father reached into the car, lifted Joey from the backseat, and handed the half-asleep child to Jessie. Looking down at Timmy, he admonished, "You be good, you hear?" Without another word, he jumped into the car and drove off in a swirl of dust.

Running after the car, Timmy called out, "Daddy! Daddy! Don't go away! Please, don't leave me here!" Out of breath, he tripped over a stump and sprawled to the ground.

Timmy laid there and cried until the sobs became whimpers. Suddenly he stiffened as a shadow covered his body. Fearfully he looked up into the face of an animal. He cringed until he realized it was a dog. He remained still, but when the dog started licking his face, he realized it wouldn't hurt him. It was a large dog, part collie and part wolf.

When Timmy stood up, the dog wagged his tail and walked off down the path. Timmy followed as the dog led him back to the cabin.

Timmy walked up the three steps onto the porch and into the house. Looking around, he saw two double beds and two rocking chairs at the far end of the room, and a crude wooden table and two long benches to the left. A kerosene lamp glowed on top of an old parlor organ.

Granny was washing Joey in a big metal tub. Looking at Timmy, she ordered, "Take off your things and get in the tub."

"I got to go to the bathroom."

"Ain't no toilet in the house. There's an outhouse out back and a slop pail on the back porch."

Timmy went to the back porch and shuddered as he used the slop bucket. Then he took off his T-shirt, shorts, shoes, and socks. Sick to his stomach, he returned to the room in his undershorts.

"Just look at you," Granny said in a stern voice. "You're some poor excuse for a boy. Your arms are too short and you're skinny." She shook her head. "Take off them shorts. Do you expect me to bathe you with your clothes on?"

As Granny bathed Timmy she detected something unusual with his genitals. "What's this?" she grabbed his scrotum and Timmy flinched. "You only got one ball? What kind of a boy are you? I'll make a real boy out of you. You'll see."

As she dried Timmy with a large rough cloth, a tall slender man walked into the room, arms filled with firewood. "This here's my husband Harry," Granny told Joey and Timmy. "Call him Uncle Harry."

Harry nodded silently at the boys, walked to the kitchen,

and stacked the wood near the stove. Harry was not much for talking. Most of the time he took care of the farm animals. Timmy only saw him at mealtimes, during which time the boys were not allowed to talk.

Over the following week, Timmy and Joey learned that life at the cabin was hard work and little play. The boys got up early, helping with the chores they were given. If they were too slow or made too many mistakes, they could expect a hard smack on the side of the head. They learned fast.

School opened a week later. It took Timmy about twenty minutes to walk through the woods to reach the road. Eventually he got used to the shadows and strange sounds.

A school bus picked him up at the end of the path. The driver greeted him. "Ain't you the kid whose folks didn't want him? Listen here, better be on time and behave yourself, or else I'll tell Granny. And you better believe me, she's crazy strict." Quietly, Timmy sat at the rear of the bus.

He was the last to get off. Walking slowly, he entered the large one-room schoolhouse. The room was filled with the noise and chatter of twenty children. He stood to one side, close to the wall, and watched, feeling very much alone.

A tall woman with wavy auburn hair approached him. Her clear brown eyes looked soft and kind. Smiling, she said, "You must be the Timmy Turner who's living with Jessie Reilly."

Timmy put his head down and nodded.

Placing her hand on his shoulder, she said, "I'm Miss Sanders, your teacher. I hope you'll be happy with us." She smiled again and took his hand. "Come with me," as she led him to her desk at the front of the room. Timmy felt shy and miserable. He looked around the room. None of the children seemed to notice him.

"Timmy, you'll sit in the first seat in the first row." She walked with him to the small desk. When he sat down, the top of the desk came to his chin. Miss Sanders explained, "You'll be in school with children of all different ages. You'll be in kindergarten and our youngest student. Children sit in different rows according to their ages. That's why your seat is here. After the eighth grade, you'll go to another school in Clara. It's a high school. Ever been in Clara?"

Timmy shook his head.

Miss Sanders pulled up a chair and sat down beside him. "Timmy, where did you live before you came here?"

Timmy bit his lip. "In Montrose, Alabama, ma'am. I lived in Montrose with my mamma and two brothers. I want to go back home to my mamma and my baby brother." Tears welled in his eyes, and he began to tremble.

Miss Sanders ran her hand through his curly brown hair. Timmy closed his eyes, and the tears rolled down his cheeks. She stroked his head gently, and the soft touch made him feel warm. He opened his eyes and managed a small smile.

"That's better. Do you know any of the children?"

Timmy shook his head. "No, ma'am."

"Well there are many boys and girls from around your area attending this school. I'm sure you'll see them from time to time on the farm. Let's see," she paused, "there's Sally. She's around six years old. Her father is Mrs. Reilly's son. He drove the school bus that brought you here today. She's a very sweet girl. And there's Fred. He's eight years old, and rather big for his age. Mrs. Reilly's grandson too." She stopped. "Oh my, I guess we don't have any boys in school around your age!"

Timmy looked at the students in the room. Some of the boys were roughhousing on the floor, and one was nailing wood together, whistling as he hammered. The noise scared Timmy. The girls were in small groups, talking to each other. He wished he could be with the girls.

And so the school year began. Nobody paid much attention to Timmy. Because he was small, the boys protested when Miss Sanders asked them to include Timmy in their games. The girls were nice to him but treated him like a baby. Only Sally, Granny Reilly's granddaughter, seemed to have any time for him.

"Don't worry," she whispered to him that first day in school. "I'll play with you when I come to visit Granny."

True to her word, Sally came to the farm that Saturday. As she greeted Timmy, she took his hand, "Let's go walking." Timmy agreed and they started off. Some distance from the house they came to an abandoned shack by the stream. Sally guided him through the door. The shack was littered with old rusty farm tools, empty cans, and broken bottles.

"Want to play house?" she asked, pushing her black curls over her shoulder.

"Uh-huh," Timmy answered, not sure what she meant.

"You be the daddy and I'll be the mommy, okay?"

Timmy was quiet for a moment. "Can't I be the mommy?" he asked.

"Don't be silly," Sally said, squinting her gray eyes at him. "Don't you know anything? You're a boy. You have to be the daddy."

"Okay," said Timmy. He looked at her pretty pink dress and then at his tattered overalls. He sighed.

After they had been playing for a while, Sally spoke up. "Don't you know what daddies are supposed to do?"

"No," Timmy answered. He remembered his father hitting his mother. He didn't think that was what Sally had in mind.

"Oh, you silly goose," Sally giggled. "Here, I'll show you."

She picked up the front of her dress. Timmy gasped when he saw the white panties covering her smooth skin.

"Now," said Sally, "take off my panties." She helped him. "That's right."

Timmy's eyes opened wide. He had never seen a girl undressed before. How smooth she was!

Sally went on. "Now, take your hand, and put your fingers in between my legs."

Timmy did as he was told.

"There, doesn't that feel good?"

Her flesh was soft and warm, slightly damp. It seemed to hold his fingers gently there. *She feels so smooth*, Timmy thought, s*he's so warm and so beautiful.*

"You're doing real good, Timmy," Sally said encouragingly. "Take off your overalls and underwear now, and I'll show you what to do next."

He pulled his hand away abruptly. "I can't," he said frantically. "I'm so ugly and you're so beautiful." He shook his head hard.

"That's okay," Sally reassured him. "You just take off your clothes."

Once again, Timmy did as he was told. "That's right." Sally nodded. "Now we can really play mommy and daddy..."

Timmy was to remember that day for the rest of his life. For the first time, he knew what he wanted to have. He knew that his body was wrong, that Sally's was right. He even thought he could feel what her body felt. For the first time, he knew what he wanted to be.

Later that night, when Timmy and Joey had been put to bed, he turned toward his brother in the dark. "Joey," he said quietly.

"What?"

"Wouldn't you like to be a girl like Sally?"

"Be a girl?" Joey replied. "Yuck! Who'd want to be a girl?"

Timmy didn't answer. He laid there in the darkness and thought how lucky girls were. Their clothes were so pretty and nice. Girls didn't play rough. They were clean and they didn't punch each other. He recalled the afternoon with Sally. He thought of her body. *If only I could be like her*, he kept thinking. *She feels so nice. Girls got it so good* . . .

That Tuesday when he got home from school, Granny took him aside immediately. "What did you do to my Sally?" she screamed in a shrill voice. "What did you do?"

Timmy swallowed hard. Terror flooded through him. He was afraid to say anything. Why did Granny want to know about Sally? She hadn't been to school the last two days. Miss Sanders said she was sick. He tried to pull away from Granny's hold. "Nothing, Granny. Honest. I didn't do nothing to her."

"That's not what I heard. Sally's appendix busted. She told the doctor you played with her private parts. Her daddy said that's what she got for letting you play with her." She wrenched him toward her. "Well, I'm going to show you what I do to boys who fool around with girls' private parts."

With a few violent jerks, she tore off Timmy's clothes. With a rope, she tied his feet and wrists together and laid his small body over the bench. She took a cow switch and began to hit him over the back and buttocks.

"I'll show you," she said every time the switch came down. "I'll show you!" She seemed to get angrier and stronger each time she hit him. Her face turned red. The welts on his bottom became thicker than fingers, and they bled. "I'll show you!"

Harry walked into the room. "What're you doing to that boy?" His face turned ashen. "Look at his back!"

"I told you what he done to our Sally. He'll never fool around with no girl again!"

"Hold on there." He pulled the switch from his wife's

hand. "Why, there's nothing left of this here switch!" Harry exclaimed in an angry voice. "You could've killed him!" He threw the switch to the floor and carried Timmy to the bed. With warm water and a soft cloth, he cleansed Timmy's wounds. Timmy lay quietly on his stomach, tears drying on his cheeks. "Now, you leave that boy alone, you hear me?" Harry turned on his heels and left the cabin.

Granny was silent for several minutes. When Harry walked out, she came to Timmy's bed. He cringed in fear, but she spoke to him in a calm voice. "I love you, Timmy," she said, "I only did what I did because I want you to grow up proper."

Left alone, Timmy wept quietly for hours in the light of the kerosene lamp at the far end of the room. The dog he had named Rex kept him company. He put his arm around the dog's neck and whispered into Rex's ear. "She keeps saying she loves me, but I just don't see how anyone can say they love you and beat you at the same time. I just don't." Through all his future years on the farm and all the beatings that came his way, Timmy never understood that any more than he did that day.

2
A Birthday Wish

"Today is a very special day," Miss Sanders stood in front of the classroom. "Does anyone know why?"

The children looked at each other with puzzled expressions. No one replied.

"Well, what day is it?"

"November twenty-sixth," Fred Reilly answered.

"And does that day mean anything to you, Timmy?" Miss Sanders smiled at him.

Timmy felt embarrassed. He lowered his head, looked at the floor, and spoke softly. "It's my birthday."

"And tell the class how old you are."

"Five years old."

"Here's a birthday cake I made for you!" Miss Sanders uncovered the plate on her desk revealing a beautiful chocolate cake with five candles and "Happy Birthday, Timmy" written in pink. "Now, make a wish and blow out the candles."

Timmy closed his eyes tight and made a wish. Opening his eyes, he blew hard until all the candles were out.

"What did you wish for?" Miss Sanders asked.

Timmy hesitated. He didn't dare tell her that he had wished to be a girl.

She smiled again. "That's all right. You don't have to tell us. They say your wishes won't come true if you tell anyone, so you're right not to say."

He clenched his fists. "My wish has got to come true. It's got to!"

Miss Sanders looked a little startled, then began cutting the cake.

Later during recess, Timmy and Miss Sanders took their usual walk by the pond. She was aware that Timmy felt rejected by his classmates. The boys didn't want Timmy to play with them, and he couldn't play with the girls. So Miss Sanders and Timmy had taken this walk every day, weather permitting, and Timmy was grateful for the attention.

While Miss Sanders sat under the cypress tree, Timmy stepped onto the ice-covered pond. But the ice was not thick enough to support his weight, and he fell through into the bitter cold water, sitting down on the pond's muddy bottom.

"Miss Sanders! Miss Sanders!"

"Oh, Timmy!" Standing at the edge, she reached and pulled him from the water. "What a terrible thing to happen, and on your birthday! Let's hurry back before you catch cold."

In the schoolhouse, he took off all his clothes except for his undershorts. Shivering, he stood by the wood stove to warm up. Miss Sanders placed her coat around him for warmth. Timmy smiled, stroked the coat, and wiggled his body so he could feel the cloth. This felt right. What a wonderful feeling having Miss Sanders' coat wrapped around his body.

Later, when he put on his own clothes, they felt wrong on his body. The brief surge of happiness was gone. He knew he wanted to wear clothes like Miss Sanders wore. They felt like they belonged on him. He knew he had to put on girl's clothes again.

The weeks between Timmy's birthday and Christmas passed quickly. Miss Sanders asked the students to tell the class their Christmas plans. "Timmy, it's your turn."

Timmy stood up at his desk, not knowing what he should say. Finally he faced the class and softly said, "I just want to be with my mother for Christmas," and sat down.

In the silence that followed, his classmates and Miss Sanders sensed Timmy's loneliness for his mother. But soon the children were involved in their games and forgot about Timmy. Except for Sally.

Timmy knew Sally felt badly about telling her parents what they had done that Saturday afternoon, when they played "mommy and daddy." He believed that if she had not been so sick the following day she would have said nothing. In fact, he believed she was the only friend he could trust.

"I'd bring your mother to you for Christmas if I could, Timmy," she said, "but I can't. I'd like to give you something special anyway. But you've got to tell me what you would want."

Blushing he whispered, "I'd like your pink organdy dress and your panties."

Sally looked at Timmy, not understanding why he would want such a thing. Finally she said, "I promise."

Christmas Eve, Sally gave him the dress and panties. Quickly, he put them in a box with red satin shoes he had found in a dump and hid the box under some straw in the barn loft. He kept smiling all that evening, until Granny told him he looked like some old coot.

Christmas Day dawned. "Boys," Granny said, "I've got a surprise for you. If you go on outside, you'll see somebody you know."

Timmy and Joey ran onto the porch, down the front steps, and on the path leading to the fence where a car had stopped. The car door opened. Timmy's heart leaped. It was his mother, holding his little brother Jimmy by the hand.

"Mamma!" Timmy ran to her, Joey was right behind him. "Mamma, Mamma, Mamma!"

"Merry Christmas, boys," she said. "It's good to see you."

"Mamma, you've come to take us home!"

"No. I'm here to bring you some presents... and to leave your little brother Jimmy with you."

"But Mamma," Timmy cried out, "you can't leave us here. You just can't!" He tugged at her skirt and started to cry.

"I can't help it. Your grandfather is very sick, and your grandmother has all she can do to take care of him. I've got to work so I can make money and send some here to pay for your keep. You don't know how lucky you are. Lots of people are standing in bread lines every day."

"I don't care. I don't have to eat. I just want to be with you!" Timmy flung his arms around her waist.

"No, Timmy." Gently, she pulled away from his arms, and shook her head. With a sympathetic look in her large brown eyes and a tone of regret in her voice, she said, "I've got to go now, R.L. is waiting for me in the car and will be impatient."

Timmy knew who R.L. was. Granny had told them that he was their new stepfather. "Oh, Mamma!"

"Now, R.L. was nice enough to bring me here so I could see you for a little while. I can't keep him waiting. You be good children, and take care of your little brother. I'm counting on you." She gave each child a brief hug. "Bye. Take care now!"

Timmy watched as she returned to R.L.'s car. He saw her drop her purse, stoop down to pick it up, and get into the car. He heard the motor start and watched the car disappear down the road.

"I have to go to the bathroom," three-year-old Jimmy announced.

"Okay, I'll show you where," Joey volunteered.

Timmy stood silently as his two brothers vanished

around the back of the house. In a few brief moments his mother had come and gone, and he was left with nothing in his life except loneliness and emptiness. He wanted to die right then and there.

Rex came to Timmy and licked his leg as if in sympathy. Timmy walked slowly down the path to where the car had parked. A glint of light from something on the ground caught his eye. Bending over, he saw that his mother's mirror and lipstick had fallen out when she had dropped her purse. Timmy picked them up, and while looking at them, felt his skin prickle with excitement. Joey and Jimmy were nowhere to be seen. He walked to the barn, and climbed up to the loft. Moving the hay covering the hidden box, he took out Sally's dress and panties and the red satin shoes, then quickly climbed back down the ladder.

Filled with excitement, he ran to the shack by the stream. Inside, he threw off his clothes and put on Sally's panties and dress. His heart pounded as he slipped the red satin high-heel shoes on his feet. Using his mother's mirror, he put lipstick on his lips. Looking down at himself, he heaved a long-drawn sigh. It had happened. Timmy had become a girl. He felt his body relax. *Oh, thank you, Timmy,* a voice said, but he knew no one was there.

Timmy thought, *I know there's a real girl inside my body, but I didn't know she could talk! I must give her a name.* He thought hard for a moment. *I'll call her Tina, that's close to Timmy.* Having been found, Tina continued to exist for the rest of Timmy's life. She made his remaining years on the farm much easier to bear.

Each morning, he rose at four to milk the cows and haul water for the animals before going to school. After school, he hoed the garden, shucked peas or corn for the table, brought the cows back to the barn, and churned butter. After finishing the last chore, he dashed to the shack by the stream and within minutes was transformed.

Tina became Timmy's solution to his lonely, solitary life. He knew that Timmy and Tina were separate people. He did not know how or why, but he was certain about the feelings that surged through his mind and body. When he slipped on girls' clothes he felt at peace. The anxiety and inner turmoil disappeared. He felt like a complete person for the first time in his life. This was his true self and identity. He had become Tina, but only Timmy was to know that for many years.

3
In Search of Home

World War II had little effect on life at the farm. Timmy, now a teenager, and his brothers continued with chores, taking on more as they grew. The farm had livestock and a truck garden, so food remained plentiful. School was much the same as before.

The sexual identity conflict within Timmy also grew. He believed Tina was living in the body of Timmy, the person that everyone else saw. He hated that body because it seemed to belong to someone else. Wearing denim overalls, doing men's work, and having a man's name were ongoing reminders of that hated identity, which increased his tension. Often he was confused as to who he was and felt disoriented. Timmy found relief from the pressure only during those moments when he wore girls' clothes and could see himself as the female he believed he was. He felt comfortable and free only when Timmy became Tina, his true self.

As he entered adolescence, Timmy's skin remained soft, and he had very little body hair. His mannerisms were not effeminate, so the boys didn't tease him. They simply left him alone. That pleased him because he wanted to be free to spend his time with the girls, who accepted his company. He watched their behavior for Tina's benefit and learned how they walked and talked. He noted their interests and little tricks of dressing and primping.

Alone in the shack by the stream he became Tina. The little shack was the dressing room permitting him to put on female clothing and enter Tina's world. By saving his pennies, he added to his makeup and wardrobe. The final decorative touch to the shack was a large mirror he found. With it he could see Tina's reflection as well as feel female.

Outside the shack Timmy was his other self, over-compensating with behavior to match the male body that had to perform its role until the real self could make things right again—until Tina, in her clothes and with her movements, could appear in the world of the dressing room.

In September of 1946, Timmy got great news. He and his brothers were to leave the farm and join his mother and R.L. Timmy's prayers to be with his mother had been answered, and he hoped that a better life was about to begin.

"I'll miss you," Miss Sanders said. "You're a very sensitive person. I think I understand a little of how you feel. I'd like to give you a copy of a poem by Edgar Allen Poe. It's called 'Alone.'"

> From childhood's hour
> I have not been as others were
> I have not seen as others saw
> I could not bring
> My passions from a common spring

Miss Sanders gave Timmy her address where he could send letters. Timmy gave his teacher a hug. "Thank you for being so kind. I don't know how I would have survived without you."

He also gave Rex a big hug and a treat, and got a lick in return.

The three boys, wearing tattered overalls, took a bus to Gainesville, Florida. The trip was uneventful, and the boys' energy level was high with expectations of going home. As they exited the bus, Timmy noticed a large lake nearby that was bordered with palm trees and moss that hung lazily from giant oaks. He thought it looked like the gateway to paradise.

Their mother, Janet, was waiting as they got off the bus, and greeted them all with hugs and kisses. Timmy thought she looked beautiful and younger than her thirty-three years. *And that's my mother.*

As their mother drove them to their new home, Timmy watched her intently, thinking, *It's really her, I'm really with my mother.* It was as if by saying that he could make himself feel close to her again, the way he thought he had felt when he was a little boy, but some childhood memories can be deceptive.

Timmy was pleased to be reunited with his mother, but he was also troubled. He had difficulty seeing her now as the mother he remembered in his mind's eye. So much had happened while they were apart that he wished he were four years old again to wipe away everything that had happened during the ten years they were apart.

"We're here, boys." She parked the car in front of a restaurant. Timmy thought they were stopping for an early lunch. Inside there was a large room with a long counter and about twenty booths. Wine, beer, and liquor to take out were sold from shelves in the front. The cash register rested on a case filled with candy, chewing gum, and nuts. In all his years, Timmy had never seen such a place. Back at the farm, a store on wheels came by once a week, and on a lucky day Granny would buy him a stick of gum or some candy. Timmy examined the candy section carefully to decide what he would select if his mother offered to let him have a treat. He paid little attention to the man behind the counter who was ringing up a sale.

After the customer left, Timmy's mother put her arms around the three boys and said, "Boys, this is your stepfather.

He wants you to call him R.L."

Timmy stared at the man towering over him. About six-feet-four, over two hundred pounds, R.L. had been a wrestler and a Marine Corps hero in World War II. Timmy thought he looked a little like John Wayne.

The boys were tense and quiet. Timmy's mother broke the silence. "R.L., this is Timmy."

"Hi." Timmy's voice was barely above a whisper. He quickly stepped behind Joe.

"And this here is Joe," she said, giving him a little shove.

"Hello," Joe said as he cleared his throat.

"And this one is Jimmy."

Jimmy stepped forward and said, "Hi!" He remembered R.L. from before he was left at the farm.

"Well, boys, it's good to have you here," R.L.'s big voice boomed out. "I hope you like the place, because you're going to be spending a lot of time here."

The boys looked at their mother, not knowing what to say.

"R.L. owns this restaurant," she explained. "I work here too, and I know you boys will want to do your share. R.L. and I live behind the restaurant. There's a garage out back, and we've added a room and a bath for you boys."

"Janet, why don't you show the boys where they'll be staying. I can manage in here for a while longer."

The boys followed their mother into a double garage and through a doorway that led to an attached room. Three cots and three small desks lined the walls. A long closet filled one end of the room, and at the other end was a toilet, a small sink, and a stall shower.

"Hey, the light goes on when you flip a switch!" Jimmy said gleefully.

"And there's hot and cold running water in the sink," Joey added. "And a real flush toilet!"

"This is really keen," Timmy managed to say. He was disappointed that he would not be living under the same roof as his mother.

"Where do we eat?" Joey asked.

"Oh gosh, you boys must be hungry after that long trip," their mother said. "Come on, we'll go back to the restaurant and you can have anything you want."

"Will we be eating together like a family?" Timmy asked.

"The restaurant is a busy place at meal times. We eat when we can."

Later in the day, their mother took the boys to town to buy clothes for school, church, work, and play. This was a new experience, and the boys had fun shopping. Timmy wandered away from the family and found himself in the girls department. He looked longingly at the clothes and tenderly touched the dresses on the racks. Tina's clothes and makeup had been left back at the farm, hidden in the shack. He didn't dare take them with him. Timmy was absorbed in thought when a voice interrupted, "Can I help you, young man?"

He turned to see a saleslady. "No, ma'am. Just looking." He left quickly to rejoin his family.

The next day the boys were enrolled in school. Joey and Jimmy went into the seventh and eighth grades, and Timmy into the ninth.

The high school was quite a contrast to the one-room schoolhouse back in Mississippi. Between classes, the halls were filled with the clamor of students. Most were well dressed, which didn't surprise Timmy when he learned that many of their fathers were tobacco growers. Timmy felt out of place, sort of like a country hick, and he missed Miss Sanders.

For about a month, the excitement of the new school and a different life style distracted him from the urge to dress as

Tina. Then the tension returned.

Timmy was embarrassed to be dressing with the boys for gym in the locker room, but as in Mississippi, they left him alone, and that was a relief. Lacking in skills and stamina, he found it hard to keep up with the other boys in gym class. Fortunately, an understanding teacher gave him assignments away from physical competition.

Whenever he could, Timmy socialized with the girls. They liked him because he wasn't as rough as the other boys, was sensitive, and seemed to understand the girls better. He frequently had a pretty girl at his side and soon became known as a ladies man. The fact that he wanted to be one of the girls remained his secret.

Timmy enjoyed girl talk about clothes and watching them put on makeup. The boys' conversations about making out with girls, erections, and wet dreams turned him off.

Timmy worked in the restaurant after school each day. During summer vacation, he washed dishes in the sweltering kitchen from early morning until the restaurant closed.

Timmy noticed that R.L. and Joey had developed a close relationship, and that his mother favored and babied Jimmy. His attempts to win attention from his mother or R.L. failed, and once again he felt ignored and alone.

"R.L.," he asked one day, "could you and me go fishing together sometime?"

"Your mother can't handle the work by herself. Someone else has got to stay here to look after the business when I'm not here. Being the oldest of the boys, you've got that responsibility." That was the end of that. Timmy didn't try again.

As summer progressed, the family situation remained the same, but Timmy felt a growing tension. He was on edge, feeling the need to be Tina.

One evening the pressure became so intense that he felt a need to get out for a while and asked his brother to cover for him. "Joey, would you mind taking over for me so I can go out for an hour or two?"

"Well, I don't know. Mom and R.L. aren't here. They'll raise Cain if they find out you went somewhere without their knowing."

"Please, Joey."

"Well . . . okay. But get back in an hour."

In the soft light of dusk Timmy walked to the lake and sat under his favorite tree. The evening breeze cooled him, and as he relaxed he began to think of Tina.

He was jolted from his thoughts by the sounds of squealing and laughter. He looked around but couldn't see anyone. The voices seemed to be coming from a nearby patch of dense shrubbery. Curious, he got up to investigate and cautiously approached the sounds. Getting closer, he recognized his mother's voice and then R.L.'s. Timmy crouched and peeked carefully through the shrubs.

"You like that, honey?" R.L. was lying on Timmy's mother. Her legs were around him.

"Hmm, you bet," she answered.

Timmy got sick to his stomach, and backed away from the shrubs. He threw up, muffling the sound with his hands. As he sat on the grass, trying to catch his breath, he felt dirty and angry. His rage turned to anguish, and he laid face down on the grass sobbing. Then with tears streaming down his face, he got up and made his way through the streets to the restaurant.

Joey was upset. "Where were you? You were supposed to be back in an hour. This place has been a mob scene."

Timmy didn't speak. He shook his head, put on the kitchen apron, and without a word began washing the dishes stacked by the sink. Joey glared at him, waiting, but Timmy was silent. Joey threw down his towel and stormed out of the kitchen.

Timmy heard his mother and R.L. come in about a half an hour later. "Any luck fishing?" Joey asked.

"I got myself a beaut," R.L. said, laughing.

Timmy couldn't contain his anger. He threw the pot in his hand onto the sink top, where it struck a stack of plates that went crashing to the floor.

"What's going on?" Timmy's mother came running into the kitchen.

Timmy was unable to answer. He stood silent and shaking.

As she looked around the room, she became angry. "What've you been doing while I was gone? I've never seen such a mess!"

Timmy was afraid to speak, fearful of what he might say.

"Hmph. I guess it's too much to expect appreciation after all I done for you."

"All you've done for me?" The rage spilled from Timmy in a scream. "All you've done for me? You dumped me like a dog for ten years, and now I'm your hired hand. You haven't been a mother to me. You don't know anything about love. Nothing! You don't know anything about being a mother..."

She cut him off. "Now you listen to me. I've suffered plenty since you were born. In The Depression I worked real hard to send that woman you called Granny five dollars a week for you and your brothers. You don't know what I've been through. Don't you talk to me like that! Why can't you be like Joey and Jimmy? What's the matter with you? People are talking, saying you're queer."

Timmy glared at her. Her lipstick was smeared and a few blades of grass were still in her hair. The fury in him mounted again.

"Go to hell! Do you think I like being the runt? I'm the way I am because of you..."

Stunned by his mother's words and blinded with fury, Timmy did not see R.L. enter the kitchen and walk toward him. R.L. swung his powerful arm, and Timmy went flying through the air, landing on his back. R.L. stood over him. "If I ever hear you talk that way to your mother again, you little bastard, I'll kill you, I swear it. You're a no-good runt!" He stomped out.

Timmy laid there, blood streaming from his nose. Hearing the ruckus, Joey and Jimmy came running. They put their arms around their mother, who was crying softly, and led her out of the kitchen.

With pain shooting through his body, Timmy slowly rose to his knees. In his mind he felt ripped apart. The one thing that had kept him going all those years on the farm was the belief that some day he would get the love from his mother he longed for. Now he knew how things really were. There was no love there, no love for him at all. He stood up and walked through the garage to his room. Timmy thought that maybe if he disappeared his mother would miss him. Maybe she and R.L. would worry about him. Suddenly he remembered that Granny had told him his father lived in Montrose. He would go there and find him. *Wait till my dad finds out my stepfather beat me up,* he thought. *Just wait. My dad will fix him.*

4
Rejected and Abused

Montrose, Alabama was about four hundred miles from Gainesville, and Timmy had no trouble hitchhiking there. Two cars and a truck later, he was within the city limits. Early-morning fog and a sunless sky did nothing to dampen his spirits. Eager with expectation, he found a pay phone.

"Timothy Turner... Timothy Turner..." He moved his finger slowly down the long list of Turners in the phone book. "Here it is!" He remembered the street Granny had mentioned. "Twenty-four Grant Avenue."

He found an open gas station and asked directions. It was easily within walking distance. Grant Avenue was deserted at that hour of the morning. The street was lined on both sides with old wooden houses badly in need of paint. Some of the porches showed broken boards, and the small patches of grass were littered with tricycles, children's toys, sheets of old newspapers, and empty beer bottles.

"Twenty-four, twenty-four," Timmy kept repeating to himself as he looked for the house. "There it is!"

He walked up the porch steps to the front door, holding his breath for a moment, and then rang the bell. It sounded loud in the morning quiet. He waited and rang again.

At the second ring, a man came to the door looking disheveled, with mussed graying blond hair and bloodshot eyes. A soiled T-shirt hung loosely over his body; his trousers fit poorly and needed laundering. He appeared to be barely awake as he peered at Timmy through the screen door.

"What do you want?" His breath was heavy with alcohol.

"Excuse me," said Timmy softly. "I'm looking for Mr. Timothy Turner."

"What you want him for?"

Timmy tried to look into the house. No one else was in sight. He looked back at the man and said nervously, "I'm his son."

"You're what?"

"I'm his son," Timmy said again, more loudly.

"You must be kidding. Who in hell are you? And what're you doing here?" The man took a few steps back in the hall and looked around as if to see if anyone was listening. He came onto the porch, closed the door quietly behind him, and towered over Timmy. "Now tell me again who you are and what you want."

"I'm looking for Timothy Turner. He's my father."

"What did you say your name was?" He looked in disbelief.

"I'm Timothy Turner, Jr."

The man sat down on the porch steps and put his face in his hands. Timmy sat down next to him, wondering what was going to happen next.

"How old are you?" the man asked in a muffled voice without raising his head.

"I'll be fifteen on November twenty-sixth. I was born in 1932."

There was a long silence. Timmy waited.

"What the hell are you doing here?" the man repeated.

"I'm looking for my father."

He looked up with an angry scowl on his face. "I know that. You said it enough times. What I'm asking is how come you're looking for your father?"

Timmy slowly ran his hand through his hair. Frightened by the anger in the man's voice, he got up and walked down the porch steps.

"All right, I'm Timothy Turner," the man admitted in a defiant tone.

Timmy turned and stared at him. He had last seen his father ten terrible years ago at the age of four, when he had been left with Granny, feeling like he was dumped in the woods like a stray dog. They looked at each other with distrust and dislike.

"You look more like a girl than a boy, except you wear boy's clothes and got a boy's hair cut. Why'd they name you after me?"

Timmy wasn't sure he had heard correctly. "What'd you say?"

"Never mind."

Moments passed. To break the silence, Timmy asked, "Is Cassandra home?"

"Shut up!" His father stood up and looked him in the eye. "Now you listen to me real careful. I'm re-married, and I got a couple of kids. My wife don't know about you or my first wife, either. I can't just walk in there and tell her, 'This here is my son by my first wife.'"

Timmy backed off. "I didn't mean any harm."

"Then do me a favor and get out of here. You can't stay here." With those words his father turned his back on Timmy and started up the steps.

"Wait! You don't understand. I've got no place to go."

"You're the one who don't understand. Go back to the farm where you was left."

"I can't," Timmy was trembling. "I've been living with my mother and stepfather in Florida this last year. Joey and Jimmy are there too. My stepfather beat..."

"Then go back to Florida!" his father interrupted. Again

he stood close to Timmy. "Now, you better understand me. Get it through that dumb head that I don't want nobody to know you even exist. Got that? Just let me be. Now get away from here."

He turned and walked back up the porch steps. As he reached the front door, it opened. There stood a young woman with a baby in her arms.

"Tim, who is that?"

"A stranger looking for directions," his father answered, blocking the door with his body. "Listen, you and the baby go on back in. I'll be there in a minute. Go ahead!" He pulled the door closed as the woman returned inside the house.

Timothy Turner walked down to his son. "All right," he said. "Your mother's brother lives just a little way from here. His name's Gus Kojack. Walk down here and make a right turn when you can't go no farther. There's a gas station. Ask anybody where Gus Kojack is. They'll tell you." With that, he went into the house, closing the front door behind him.

Confused and sad, Timmy followed his father's directions. He felt more alone than ever. What had just happened fueled the turmoil of Tina within him. He thought, *If I were a girl, a real girl like Tina, they'd take care of me.* The urge to wear women's clothes welled up like a sudden storm. He squared his shoulders and walked a little faster.

The men at the gas station all knew his uncle, and a customer offered him a ride. "Gus Kojack? Sure, I know where that is. I'm heading that way in a little while. I'll drive you if you want to wait."

Less than an hour later, Timmy was walking up the path to his uncle's house. When no one answered the doorbell, he turned to walk away. He could not repeat another scene like the one he just had with his father.

"Yes, what is it?" A man had come to the door.

Timmy spun around. "I'm Timmy Turner," he said quietly. "I'm looking for my Uncle Gus."

"You must be Janet's son! Well, what do you know? Come in, come in." He opened the door wide. "I'm your Uncle Gus. Nellie," he called out, "come here. We've got company."

A middle-aged woman with a kind face appeared. She looked at Timmy, then at her husband.

"This is my sister Janet's son," Gus said with a smile.

Nellie smiled warmly. "Where's your mother?" she asked.

"In Gainesville, Florida, ma'am."

"You're here alone?" Gus asked.

"Yes sir, you see, sir, I . . . well, I had some trouble with my stepfather and left home."

"Oh, well, come on in. Nellie, give him some towels. You go on upstairs and wash up, and Nellie will fix you something to eat."

Timmy didn't realize how hungry he was. He cleaned his plate and was given seconds without asking. Aunt Nellie smiled her approval.

"We're short on space," she said when Timmy had finished, "but you can sleep on the porch until we can make some plans for you. We'll phone your mother and let her know you're here, so she won't worry."

That next week, Timmy ate a lot and slept more deeply than he ever remembered. The enclosed porch was comfortable, and he discovered how pleasant some privacy could be. His aunt and uncle didn't know about Tina, but he felt accepted for himself and felt good about that for the first time in his life.

He met his mother's family and learned that his grandfather had died and his grandmother was ill. His three uncles and two aunts kept him busy doing odd jobs for them, and they paid him for the work. He liked them and felt at ease. Timmy Turner had a family.

One night about two months later, while he was asleep on the porch, the noise of a chair being bumped into woke him up. His Uncle Gus was standing by the bed.

"Shhhh," he said, putting his finger to his lips. Timmy smelled the whiskey. Uncle Gus was drunk.

Timmy sat up in bed. He drew the blankets tightly around his body. Instinctively he felt threatened.

"Shhhh," Uncle Gus said again. He sat down on the bed next to Timmy. "I kept thinking about you out here all alone on the porch, and how lonely you must be feeling all by yourself."

Timmy turned his head to avoid his uncle's breath. "I'm not lonely. I'm just fine."

"Shhhh," Gus said. He moved the blankets away from Timmy's shoulders and got in under them. "Don't be scared. I'm not going to hurt you."

He was not strong enough to fight off his uncle. He wouldn't call for help because he didn't want his aunt to be hurt, and he was embarrassed by his uncle's behavior. He submitted.

Sometime before dawn, his uncle woke up and stumbled out of the room. Shortly after that, Timmy dressed. He was in the kitchen when his aunt came down.

"I've been thinking," he said. "Tomorrow is my birthday, and it's Thanksgiving. Maybe it's time for me to swallow my pride and go home. Maybe I'll even go back to school."

"That's a good thing to do!" she said. "You're a smart boy. You should get your education. And your mother will be so happy to see you. I know it's not the easiest thing in the world to have a stepfather, but he's really a good man." She hugged him. "You know you're always welcome back here if you want to return," she added, smiling warmly at him.

A little over twelve hours later, Timmy arrived back in Gainesville.

5
The Spiritual Search

R.L.'s restaurant was crowded. Timmy looked through the window and tried to catch his mother's eye, but she didn't notice him. When R.L. and his brothers went into the kitchen he stood by the door and waved to her. She motioned with her hand for him to wait outside. A few minutes later she joined him, and they went out back where they couldn't be seen.

"What are you doing here?"

"I've come back home," Timmy said. His mother seemed annoyed to see him. He hadn't expected that. "I'm sorry I cussed you. I hope you'll forgive me."

She continued as though she hadn't heard him. "You can't stay here." She looked around nervously. "R.L. said he'd skin you alive if he saw the likes of you around here again."

"But you're my mother! This is my home. I want to be with you." His mother's expression did not change. "I want to go back to school," he added, hoping that would help.

"Well, I got news for you. Me and your brothers had a talk, and we decided you're no good, like your father. We're doing just fine here without you, and we aim to keep it that way."

Timmy was stunned. "But I'm your son, too! Don't you understand that I need you? All my life I've just wanted to be with you. I love you!"

"Now you listen to me. R.L. and I worked hard to get

what we got. When he first bought this place, it was a little liquor store with two gas pumps. I started fixing sandwiches to take out. It took a long time to get it fixed up into a good-looking restaurant. There's my blood in this business, and I'm not going to lose it because of the likes of you." Her voice was low and harsh. "Do you hear me?"

Timmy's worst fears had come true. His mother would have nothing to do with him. He felt his years of prayer and hope dissolving into nothing. He turned and walked away.

"Timmy."

He stopped. *Thank God,* he thought, *she's calling me back.*

"Here." She handed him a crumpled bill. "It's a ten."

He stared at her. She pushed the money into his hand and hurried back into the restaurant.

Alone and totally miserable, he headed toward the highway and walked blindly along the side of the road. He wished a car would run him over.

"Hey, Timmy."

He spun around. A driver he had seen at R.L.'s leaned out of the cab of his truck.

"Want a ride?" he asked.

Timmy shrugged his shoulders. "Why not?" He climbed in beside the driver.

"Where to?"

"Where you going?"

"Montrose."

"That'll be fine." He didn't think he would see his father or Uncle Gus. It was a large town.

The drive was uneventful. Timmy was emotionally drained and physically exhausted. He put his head back and fell asleep. A tap on his shoulder woke him.

They had arrived at the outskirts of Montrose and the driver said, "There's somebody I want you to meet." He pulled in at a truck stop with some cabins in the back and introduced Timmy to the owner. Timmy was hired to clean up, and help out in the restaurant in exchange for room and board.

A month passed quickly. Timmy worked hard, and the tips were good. He bought some makeup along with a satin nightgown and shoes. Every night after working hours, he would sit alone in his room dressed as Tina. With the radio playing soft music, he learned to smoke cigarettes with graceful gestures and imagined himself popular and successful, the most beautiful woman in the world. Being Tina seemed to heal him, help him feel strong again, and allow his horrible memories of what had happened to fade.

During that month, he avoided going into Montrose. He did not want to run into his father or Uncle Gus. But as Christmas approached, he yearned to be with his family. He decided to go to his mother's sister, Ellen. She even looked like his mother.

"Timmy!" his Aunt Ellen exclaimed when she answered the doorbell. "Timmy, how good it is to see you! Come on in."

She looked past his shoulder when he walked in. "Where's the rest of your family?"

"My family?"

"Well, yes. Your mother called last week. We're going to have a family reunion. I thought you'd settled your differences with her and came with them."

At that moment, the bell rang. "My Lord, that must be them. You make yourself comfortable while I get the door."

Timmy went into the kitchen, where he could hear what was happening but not be seen.

"Janet, R.L., boys, Merry Christmas!"

Timmy slowly opened the door a crack and peeked out. There they were, their arms filled with packages.

"Timmy just got here," Ellen went on.

"Timmy?" he heard his mother say. "Timmy is here?"

"If he's here, I'm leaving," R.L. said flatly.

"Please, it's Christmas," Ellen said.

Timmy slipped out the back door. He would not wait for the confrontation. He walked aimlessly for hours on the empty streets of Montrose. Except for an occasional group of people on their way to a Christmas celebration, he saw no one. The houses decorated with wreaths and warm lights made him feel even more isolated and alone.

Everything seemed hopeless. He had no one to be with, no place to go. But Tina stayed within him, hidden from everyone. Even so, he could not continue to live this way, a life of isolation. He saw a Baptist church. He would go in, make his peace with God, and end it all.

There were just a few people in the simple church. Timmy sat in a pew at the back of the church and watched families arrive for Christmas services. He sang the hymns and half-listened to the sermon, his mind wandering back to the church in Mississippi. Granny had made him go every Sunday. At Granny's church the preacher would shout at the congregation, jab his fingers at them, and pound his fists on the lectern as he delivered the sermon. Members of the congregation would shout "Hallelujah!" and "Amen!" as the preacher talked. The air there was always hot and stuffy, and paper fans advertising the funeral home circulated unpleasant odors that nauseated him.

This church was not like that. It was subdued, quiet, and peaceful. It made him feel better. When the minister finished the sermon and the service concluded, Timmy left the church to think about what to do next.

"Son."

He kept walking; no one he knew ever called him "son." He was no one's son.

"Son." He felt a hand on his shoulder. There stood a middle-aged man and woman. "My wife and I...that is...we wondered if you were alone?"

"Yes I am."

"Well, my wife and I thought if you were alone, you might want to join us for dinner at our hotel? I'm Bob Spencer. This is Aileen, my wife."

The man was tall, slender, gray-haired, and had a pleasant face. His wife was also tall and slender. Gray hair softly framed her face. She had bright blue eyes and a warm smile. She reminded Timmy of his teacher, Miss Sanders, who had been so kind to him.

Timmy joined them for a pleasant and relaxing dinner at the hotel, during which time he told them about studying the Bible when he lived with Granny and Uncle Harry. While having dessert, the Spencers looked at each other, and Aileen Spencer nodded.

"Son," Mr. Spencer said, "we sell Bibles and could use someone to help us. You know about the Bible, and you're from this part of the country. Would you like to come with us?"

Pleased, Timmy agreed. For the next two and a half years, the Spencers became Timmy's adopted family, and he developed a close relationship with them. Together they travelled from town to town, selling Bibles and religious articles to little shops and homes door-to-door. Timmy's deep Southern accent and knowledge of the Bible helped increase sales.

Timmy's nights were spent at boarding houses and cheap hotels. As busy as he was with work, there were times when tension built within him, mostly at night. Timmy would go to his room, take out his women's clothes, and become Tina for a few blessed periods of peace. The Spencers never found out about Tina.

Timmy did ask them questions about the Bible. "As a Baptist, am I correct in believing in Fate and Destiny? I mean, God predetermines whatever events come to pass?"

"That's our understanding," the Spencers replied in unison.

"Could you explain Genesis to me? I know it's the first book of the Bible that talks about creation and the beginning of the universe as created by God, but I am confused about the creation of man and woman, and male and female differences." That was as close as Timmy could approach them regarding his confusion perceiving himself as a woman trapped in a male body, and the feeling he was different from other males.

Bob Spencer explained. "Some early theological interpretation of the Scriptures was that Adam originally had two faces and two body fronts, and eventually Eve was formed by splitting apart Adam. Then both the Midrash (early Hebrew Bible) and Talmud (Jewish law) imply, as I understand it, that Adam and Eve were like Siamese twins joined back to back. Then there is the version that Eve was created from Adam's rib while he slept. Different cultures have different interpretations about the creation of Adam and Eve. Scientists are investigating biological, psychological, and cultural factors regarding the bisexuality of humans. At least, that's what I learned when I thought about becoming a minister."

Timmy tried to digest all this information. Just maybe, God predetermined him to be two people, both male and female. Maybe Tina was like his Siamese twin, taking her position in his brain and soul. But she dominated him because she controlled his brain and soul. How could he explain this situation to anyone, even the Spencers. Is this his fate, his destiny as a good Baptist? Why him? Even Siamese twins are surgically separated to survive as individuals.

In the summer of 1950, the Spencers had to return to

Cortland, New York, to take care of Mrs. Spencer's sister. "My wife and I would like your permission to meet with your family before we part," Mr. Spencer said.

Timmy was reluctant to take them to Gainesville to meet his parents but respected their wishes. Nervously, he waited in the car while the Spencers went into R.L.'s restaurant. About a half an hour later, they came out.

"R.L. and your mother agreed to let you come back," they said, obviously pleased with the meeting.

Timmy cried and thanked them for all they had done. Sadly, he waved goodbye as they drove away.

Life at R.L.'s restaurant took on a pattern very quickly. Timmy hardly spoke to anyone, and about the only conversations they had were to tell him what to do. He was kept busy from morning to night, treated more like one of the hired help than a member of the family. The restaurant menu had expanded, and barbecue was its specialty. Each morning Timmy built the fire and barbecued about twenty hams and shoulders of pork. After school he worked as a waiter and later helped with the kitchen clean up.

Timmy found it difficult readjusting to school after being away for so long. He was almost eighteen and only in the ninth grade. He felt awkward and stupid, especially because Joey and Jimmy were in the eleventh and twelfth grades. After a month he told R.L. he wanted to quit school.

"If you quit school, you can't live here."

"But why?"

"Because I said so. And what I say goes in this place."

Nonetheless Timmy left school. He got a job delivering milk in the early morning. R.L. realized he could still use Timmy evenings in the kitchen, so he let him stay. In November, when Timmy turned eighteen, he became a linesman for the state highway department.

Timmy knew that his family still did not accept him and

probably never would. It hurt, and he wondered what he could do about it. *Maybe things would improve if I could find a way to make them proud of me.*

One day he heard R.L. bragging about being a hero during the Second World War. It was 1951. War was raging again, this time in Korea. Timmy decided to join the army. He would become a man and come back to the approval of his family.

6
Eunuchs and Geishas

On a rainy February day in 1951, Timmy boarded a bus for Jacksonville, Florida, heading for the nearest army recruiting center. He felt mixed emotions of fear, pride, and determination. Frightened, because he did not think he was man enough. He perceived himself as only being part man and his real self as a woman, yet he was about to enter a man's world. Proud because he was going to serve his country, and determined to become a good soldier whether he was Timmy or Tina.

Nevertheless, anxiety mounted during the hour-long ride. He could not dress as Tina on an army post. If he couldn't do that the tension and strain might become unbearable. But he was eighteen, he reminded himself, and one way or another he was going to start his own life, and learn to live with his dual identity.

Arriving at the bus terminal, he walked to the recruiting office. "I want to join the army," he told the sergeant.

"You have to be eighteen or have your parents' written approval," was the prompt reply.

"But I'm over eighteen."

Skeptical, the sergeant looked him over. Then he handed him a form to fill out and directed him to the back room, where he undressed to be weighed.

"You're not heavy enough," the sergeant said.

"How much do I have to weigh?" Timmy was disappointed.

"At least one hundred eleven. Even then it will be tough on you in boot camp."

Timmy stepped off the scale, dressed, and said, "I'll be back."

Three days later he returned.

"Back so soon?"

"Yep. I've done nothing but eat bananas and drink malteds since I left here." Timmy made a face. "I never want to see or eat either one again."

"What's the rush to join the army?"

"All I ever hear is my stepfather bragging about being a war hero. I want to show him I can be a good soldier, too."

"Who is your stepfather?"

"R.L. Cooper."

"No kidding! The guy who owns the R.L. Restaurant in Gainesville?"

"Yes."

"Well, what do you know? I've been at his place lots of times. That's where I must have seen you. I knew you looked familiar. Go on back and I'll weigh you. I'll give you a break. Keep your clothes on, that should help."

Anxiously Timmy stepped on the scale.

The sergeant shook his head. "You're still three pounds under, and that's with your clothes on."

Discouraged, Timmy started to leave.

"Turner, come here," the sergeant called. Startled, Timmy walked back to the desk.

"Here." He handed Timmy some papers. "Good luck, soldier," he said with a smile.

Timmy stood there in disbelief.

"Everything okay?"

"Yes, sir!" Timmy snapped back with a grin.

"You'll join the group that's gathered just outside the

office. It leaves in an hour for Fort Jackson in South Carolina."

An hour later, Timmy and the others piled into an open army truck and headed for the post. It had begun to rain, and by the time they arrived they were all wet, cold, and hungry. Timmy didn't mind.

The first few days at Fort Jackson were spent in a rush of getting uniforms, being assigned to barracks, taking tests, and getting used to the routine. Timmy was attached to the 315th Signal Construction Battalion.

The opening weeks of boot camp kept him so busy he seldom thought of Tina. Telephone personnel taught his unit how to put up poles and string wire. He was learning man's work.

The men showed a loyalty and concern for each other that was entirely new to Timmy. They realized that he had some physical limitations due to his slight build and they helped him. He felt he belonged to a group for the first time.

Nevertheless, inwardly he saw himself as more of an observer in this man's world than one of the men. The men shared a deep male sexuality that was mysterious to him. Their main topics of conversation were women and sex, subjects that never crossed Timmy's mind—at least not in the same way. Their sexual needs had a shared urgency to them that seemed to bind them. Probably because they could not imagine him feeling otherwise, they included him in their male community of friends.

Phil, who had the bunk next to his, became his buddy. Phil left college after two years, and the army drafted him. He and Timmy were the same height, but Phil was very muscular. They hit it off right away.

Contrary to his expectations, Timmy was attracted to the army. He enjoyed the challenge of hard work and the discipline, and he believed in the demands of loyalty and courage.

Dressing as a soldier gave him particular pleasure. His care about his appearance resulted in a recommendation for "Soldier of the Month." The joy he felt was genuine; he had never received special recognition for anything before.

At the end of the six weeks, he was promoted to P.F.C. and given a three-day pass. His first impulse was to show himself off to his family, and he took the bus to Gainesville.

He found only Jimmy in the restaurant. "Where is everybody?"

"In Ocala."

"Ocala?"

"Yeah. They're buying Joe a new Buick. Business had been real good, and they wanted to give him a present. Did you know he manages the place now?"

Timmy's face fell. "Good for Joe," he managed to say. "Tell the folks I dropped by, will you? I'm off to Korea soon, so I won't see you for a while."

"Right," Jimmy said. "Lots of luck."

It's hopeless, Timmy thought. *No matter how hard I try, I can't belong to my own family.*

Two days remained of his three-day pass. The men at the base would laugh if he went back ahead of time. He decided to go to Myrtle Beach, a resort area not far from Fort Jackson.

The bus was crowded, but he eventually found a seat beside an attractive young blonde.

"Where are you headed?" she asked when he had sat down.

He told her.

"That's where I live. You stationed at Fort Jackson?"

"Yep."

"So was my husband."

"Where is he now?"

She turned her head away. "He was killed in Korea."

"I'm sorry," Timmy said. "I'm off to Korea myself soon."

"I hope what I said didn't upset you!"

"Don't let it worry you." The possibility of getting killed had never entered Timmy's mind.

"Are you married?" she asked suddenly.

"Married? Not yet." That thought had never entered Timmy's mind either. *Living as a man but thinking he was Tina was hard enough. How could he ever be a husband? How could Tina ever marry a woman?*

She interrupted his thoughts. "I've got a son."

"A son?" He was surprised. She seemed so young.

She nodded. "He's twelve. His name is Andy."

"He's some lucky boy to have a mother like you. But you sure don't look old enough to have a son that age."

She smiled. "My name is Peggy Jennings."

"Pleased to meet you. I'm Timmy Turner."

"When do you think you'll be leaving for Korea, Timmy?"

"In about a week, probably." *A twelve-year-old-son,* he thought. *He's only six years younger than me. She must be at least twenty-eight, but she looks twenty. I bet she's a wonderful mother.*

Once again her voice broke into his thoughts. "Would you like me to write to you?"

"Would you?" He was almost the only person in his barracks who never got mail.

"I'd really like to."

When they arrived in Myrtle Beach, Peggy invited him to meet her parents and her son. He felt comfortable and relaxed with all of them, and they asked him to stay for dinner. He spent as much of the next two days as he could with Peggy. She gave him a snapshot of herself when he left and promised to write.

"Wow! She looks like Doris Day!" Phil said. "You got good taste, buddy."

Timmy smiled, pleased, but said nothing. He had never had a girlfriend before, and he wasn't sure how he felt. Peggy was more like Tina's friend than his. His feelings toward her were very confused.

They shipped out a few days later for San Francisco, from where they would sail overseas. One-day passes were distributed.

"I'm going to get a tattoo," Phil announced. "Come on, Timmy, you've got to get one too. Let's go!"

Flustered, not sure whether he liked the idea or not, he went with Phil to a seedy tattoo parlor near the docks. He chose the design of a heart with a ribbon around it, a dagger through it, and the words "U.S. Army."

As the form was painfully taking shape on his arm, he thought he heard Tina's voice: *Are you making me the tattooed lady?* But he chose to ignore it.

The next morning, fifteen hundred men boarded the S.S. Marine Addrer. A week later they landed in Yokahama. In rapid succession, they turned in their gear, were each given a pack and an M-1 rifle, piled into landing ships, and sent to the combat zone.

Before long they saw the dark sky lit with the streaks of shells. The roar of the big guns and explosions got gradually closer. They were ordered to slide down a grass rope and wade to shore. Timmy almost collapsed under the weight of his pack. He stayed close behind Phil. They pushed through barbed wire at the shoreline and climbed into trucks. Through darkness lit only by explosives, the convoy rolled to a camp high up on a hill. He collapsed on his cot and slept a dreamless, exhausted sleep.

Timmy's job was to string communications wire on the poles that dotted the landscape. Working with a partner, he climbed the poles with a roll of field wire on his back.

Every day for the next month the sound of explosions grew nearer. They joked about it, but the men were tense.

One day the sounds were so close that Timmy could feel the pole tremble. Suddenly a shell landed nearby. The concussion knocked his partner off the pole, and he pulled Timmy down with him. He fell hard to the ground and landed on the roll of field wire. It cut through his clothes and pierced his right testicle. The pain was blinding; he screamed once, and lost consciousness.

He awoke on a hospital train on its way to Pusan, where he was examined upon arrival. The doctors wanted to remove the testicle. It was undescended, which Timmy knew, and probably giving him more trouble than it was worth now that it was damaged. Timmy refused. The injury no longer hurt, and the wound was healing; he wanted to get back to his buddies.

When Timmy returned to duty at the front, he was assigned to deliver messages to the 7th, 13th, and 24th divisions. The jeep he drove from place to place seemed able to handle anything it met on or off the road. Timmy liked to drive; he was a good driver and knew it. His hands were firm on the wheel as the jeep bounced over rocks and through ruts. He was in control.

After a few months, he was ordered to report to a Brigadier General Coleman, commanding officer of the 8th Corps Artillery. General Coleman was a handsome man with flaming red hair and a handlebar mustache, who stood well over six feet tall. "Turner, I hear you're a good driver. I'd like you to drive for me."

"Yes, sir." He could barely keep the grin off his face.

"And when I see you again," the general added, "I want you to be wearing corporal's stripes on that sleeve."

"Yes, sir!"

Driving for the general was both exciting and dangerous, dust or slippery mud in the warm weather, frozen ruts and slick ice in the winter. Often they were in the mountains, speeding across rock-strewn roads quickly cut out of the earth. Wherever they went, shells exploded continually around them. Timmy's pride grew; he could get through anything.

The general flew to a conference above the Thirty-eighth Parallel, and Timmy went with him as his driver. There he met many men high in the army command, including General Matthew Ridgeway. He was treated well and, for the first time, with respect.

But no matter what he was doing or how he felt, he never lost the nagging wish to prove himself to his mother and R.L. He wanted them to see him as a success; maybe then they would change their minds. Tina, too, was a persistent presence, but she seemed content for the moment to stay quiet under Timmy's pride.

In March 1952, he and his company had been at the front for six months. They were sent to Yokahama for their period of rest and recreation. R&R meant one thing to most soldiers: sex. After six months without women, they were the major thought on every man's mind. They were for Timmy, too, but the reasons were different. He longed to be with someone soft and feminine. He wanted perfume and sweet smells, makeup, and women's clothes. The thought of silk next to his skin excited and pleased him. Tina may have been quieted, but she never really went away.

With dread and excitement, he went with Phil and a few others to a geisha house. He knew he would be among women's things, and that excited him, but he also knew he would probably be expected to have sex, and he dreaded that.

The geisha house was in a small Western-style private home. The living room had been turned into a bar and at the front was a small raised platform. When the group of soldiers came in, a fat woman wearing a heavy silk kimono in turquoise and gold clapped her hands.

Twenty young girls promptly paraded out and were offered to the men. All were pretty and seemed shy; they giggled often from behind their fans. Most of the girls were fairly short, a few were rather fat, and one or two looked very stern; the tallest carried a small whip.

Timmy chose the tiniest, shortest girl for himself. Together they went to a small cubicle-like room that held little more than the bare essentials: a bed, a bureau with a mirror over it, one chair, and a water pitcher with a basin and several towels. The girl spoke only a few words of English. She smiled at him, and leaned over to open his belt.

"No." He pushed her hand away.

She smiled again, stood up, and began to take off her robe.

"No!" Timmy stopped her.

She looked at him, still smiling, "You want talk?"

"Oh, no! Please..." Timmy was very embarrassed.

She moved to the bed and laid down; the smile never left her face. "You," she said, gesturing over her body, "you like do, yes?"

Greatly relieved, Timmy said, "Yes..."

He went to her and opened her robe all the way. He looked at her body and touched it with his fingertips. The smooth skin was cool. She laid still as he moved his hands over her. He felt no tension, no excitement, only a pleasure he could not identify. Then he realized what he wanted to do.

With gestures and simple words, he got her to remove her robe. He took off his own clothes and slipped the silken fabric over his body. He managed to make her understand that he wanted lipstick and perfume, and she found these for him in a bureau drawer. Relaxed and confident, his flesh tingling under the light silk, Timmy admired himself in the mirror. Tina was there.

The geisha on the bed watched, nodding encouragingly. He joined her wearing her clothes and makeup, wanting to stroke her body, and to feel her breasts, wishing they were on his body. She complied, and though he had no erection, he enjoyed the sensations. He was Tina, and he felt happy.

It was with a sense of wrongness that almost brought tears to his eyes when Timmy put on his own clothes and joined his buddies.

As they were leaving, Phil pointed to a group of five geishas standing together in a corner of the room. "Would you believe," he said, "that those geishas there are men?"

"What? What do you mean?"

"Male geishas for queers. They either come out dressed as women or they work as male geishas, depending." He shot Timmy a look. "Don't you know about homosexuals?"

"Well, I... I just didn't know that men ever dressed like women." Timmy was surprised. He thought he was the only man in the world who wanted to dress as a woman.

"They don't always dress like girls. Some of them do, just sometimes."

"Do the guys... I mean, do the male geishas pretend they're women when they're having sex with another guy?"

"Listen, Timmy, I'm not into these things," Phil responded. "I think there are some queers who have sex with each other without getting all dressed up like women. The ones who like to dress like women, what're they called? Transvestites! Yeah that's it."

Timmy's mind raced. He wasn't homosexual. He couldn't be. Sex with a man turned him off completely, left him cold, feeling revolted. He recalled how horrible it was being molested by Uncle Gus. He could imagine himself having sex only if he were Tina. But he had a man's body. It was impossible, and the whole idea of sex as Timmy or Tina turned him off.

Phil continued. "There are eunuchs in Lucknow, in India, who really think they're women. I read about them in college. They have their genitals cut off and get their pubic hair reshaped, so they'll look like a woman with a vagina. Isn't that something?"

Shock and surprise shot through Timmy's mind. *It was possible, then, to have a woman's sex organs if you were a male! Somehow I could have a woman's body after all. I could be a woman! Then I could be Tina all the time!* The sudden realization was so great he laughed and slapped Phil on the back.

"Hey, what's up, buddy?" Phil smiled and looked confused.

"Nothing, nothing... that's just a funny story, about those eunuchs."

The two walked on together, arms across each other's shoulders, to continue with their night on the town.

After his leave, Timmy returned to the front for three more months. By June 1952, he had earned thirty-six points, was awarded the Korean ribbon, a United States ribbon, two battle stars, and three campaign stars. His overseas tour was finished, and he received orders to return to the States.

He didn't realize that the night in the geisha house had planted a seed that would take many years to bloom and change his life forever.

7
A Hero's Welcome

When the troops arrived in San Francisco, they were given a heroes' welcome: cheering crowds, flags and banners, headlines, even a parade. Timmy felt pride for all of his comrades, and he was especially proud of himself for having made it in the man's world of war and soldiering.

R.L. and his mother were in his thoughts often, and he desperately wanted them to see him now. Timmy had sent them gifts from overseas, and his mother also received a check from his pay each month. From the contents of her few letters, he believed they were written just to keep the benefits coming.

When the troop train stopped in Chicago, he chose to go directly to South Carolina and see Peggy. She had written to him faithfully, while he rarely heard from his family.

A smile lit his face at the sight of Peggy standing inside the Myrtle Beach bus terminal. Someone who really wanted to see him was waiting for him. "Timmy, you look wonderful!" She flung her arms around his neck, he gave her a big hug, and they kissed.

"You're beautiful, Peg, really beautiful." He held her away from him and grinned. "I almost wore out your picture showing it to the guys in Korea."

Arm in arm, they walked to her car. She smiled at him as he opened the door for her, and again they kissed. Timmy drove, his thoughts focused on Peggy, when suddenly it occurred to him: *they looked good together, and she acted as though she loved him. He liked her family and her son, Andy, and they got along well.* He pulled the car to the curb and stopped the motor.

"Is something the matter, Timmy?"

He took her hand. "Peg, will you marry me?"

"Timmy! Are you serious?"

"Yes, of course I mean it. Will you marry me?"

Peggy was speechless. She nodded, then threw her arms around him, and said, "Yes! Yes!"

It was that simple. They were married that afternoon by a justice of the peace in Andrews, South Carolina.

After a small party with Peg's parents and her son, Timmy and Peggy drove to a motel to spend their wedding night. There, Timmy told her he had orders to report to Fort Ruker in Enterprise, Alabama. "Can we leave soon so I can get you and Andy settled?"

"You mean you're not going to stay in South Carolina?"

"I can't, I'm still in the army, and I have orders to report to Fort Ruker."

"Timmy, I . . . well, I can't leave here."

"You can't? Why not?"

Peggy was upset. She sighed deeply. "Timmy, Andy has a problem. If he's not with either my folks or me he panics. When he's someplace he doesn't know, the same thing happens. He gets upset and has difficulty breathing. It's been that way ever since his father was killed. They were very close. I can't take him away."

Timmy put his face in his hands, "We married out of love for each other, and now I learn we must live apart. Why didn't you tell me you couldn't leave South Carolina?"

"Honestly, Timmy, I thought you'd be stationed here." Tears filled her eyes. "I thought we'd settle here when you got out."

"Really, Peggy..." Timmy stood up and began to pace. He thought about the situation. The image of himself as a married man included Peggy there beside him, waiting for him at the end of the day in a home they shared together. Andy was in that scene, too. Most of all, Timmy had hoped that with Peg's help, with her warmth and understanding, he would eventually be able to have normal sex. But if he only saw her once or twice a month...

"Timmy, you do understand, don't you?" she pleaded.

He couldn't answer her.

"We can get our marriage annulled." She was crying.

"No. We'll work it out." He didn't want to shatter the dream so quickly. Peggy was the only secure thing he had in his life.

"I can come visit you sometimes for a couple of days." Timmy returned to the chair and she sat at his feet, her head on his knees. "And you can come up here whenever you get a pass."

"Don't worry, honey." He stroked her soft blonde hair. "We'll manage. You don't know how much I need you."

Her eyes looked into his for a long moment. "Let's go to bed," she said softly. She stood and slowly began to remove her dress, looking at him expectantly.

Oh, God, he thought, and started to panic. "I'll take a shower first," he said. He had to think about what to do, and stall for time.

He found Peggy lying in the bed. Her arms opened to him and he got in beside her. He held her naked body against his own and kissed her, but he felt no sexual arousal except the pleasant sensation of her smooth, soft skin.

"You're not..." she said, and her hand moved to his penis.

"Don't," he said, taking her hand away. He could not stand having his genitals touched.

He kissed her again, her mouth, her shoulder; he put his lips on her breast. But he did not have any sexual reaction, nothing. After a moment with his eyes closed, he pretended he was a woman making love; he felt like Tina. It was strange, it was frightening, but he felt the first stirring of arousal. Not enough, though, not enough. And it was not what he really wanted. His eyes always closed, seeing himself as Tina lying with Peggy, he kissed and caressed her body, finally bringing his mouth between her legs. It was satisfying to him somehow, and her sounds and movements made him know she was fulfilled. But he had not yet had an orgasm. If Peggy wondered about this kind of lovemaking, she didn't show it or say anything.

In the remaining few days they had together, this was always how they made love. Peggy did not mind, and Timmy was relieved. He enjoyed arousing her, felt pleased that it seemed to be enough for her, and he felt a mystifying happiness that Tina was making love.

Timmy finally reported at Fort Ruker. He came to hate the endlessly damp overbearing heat and was totally bored. He disliked guard duty, which happened often and kept him in the blazing hot sun. His job of checking radios did not interest him. He wanted to see his buddies from Korea, particularly Phil. The monotonous daily routine made him yearn for the unpredictability of the front lines.

Timmy missed Peggy. At last, another human being cared for him. She wrote a letter daily, and once a month she would visit him for a few days. But there remained a void in his life, an empty space that made him feel off balance. Tension began to grow, and Tina's presence grew almost as if to fill that space. The desire to dress as Tina began occupying his thoughts. He often recalled Phil's story of the eunuchs who had their genitals removed.

Timmy got a pass to get off the base whenever he could,

visiting the nearby town of Enterprise. Aside from a movie house, a pool hall, and a diner, there wasn't much to do. He disliked the rough, loud maleness of the pool hall, and he didn't much care for the movies. But he felt comfortable in the diner, which was run by the owner, his two sons, and daughter. With a cup of coffee, he would sit at the counter and pass time chatting with the sons and daughter and watching the activity. He had told them about R.L.'s place in Florida. They seemed to like having him around.

One night the owner's daughter, Darlene, approached him. She was just sixteen and not particularly attractive, with long black hair pulled straight back over her ears revealing a high forehead. Timmy thought of her as a skinny kid. She rarely looked at anyone directly with her small brown eyes.

"Take me home, Timmy? It's okay for me to leave now."

"Sure, why not?" He slid off the counter stool, waved good night to her father, and walked to the car with her.

They made the trip in silence. When he stopped at her house, she suddenly said, "Timmy, marry me?"

Timmy laughed. "Sure that's a great idea. I'll call my wife and tell her you proposed to me, and would she mind if I were married to both of you."

"I'm serious, Timmy," she said, leaning back against the car door, her hands clenched tightly in her lap. She spoke in a low, tense tone. "I just got to get out of this place before I go bananas. I hate my folks. My brothers are always picking on me. Please divorce your wife and marry me. Please, Timmy, I can't take it any more staying here."

"Take it easy, Darlene, take it easy." His voice was softened by sympathy. "You know I can't marry you, and we certainly can't live together. They'd run me out of town, and I'd get in trouble at the base. We could go to a movie once in a while? How about that? Would that help any?"

"Oh, yes, Timmy." She exhaled deeply and her shoulders

relaxed. "We'll have good times, you'll see."

Because her family saw her as the baby and trusted Timmy, they did not mind when he began driving her home from the diner and sometimes taking her to the movies.

She flirted and primped for him, which made him feel a little better about Peggy's absence. Being kidded by the men at the base about jailbait made him feel part of a shared male community again. All in all, with a wife back home, he thought things looked pretty respectable and good in his life.

However, Tina never left him. Neither did the tension. But she was invisible to everyone else, and he tried to get by on that.

Then a letter from Peggy arrived. Andy was getting worse. She could no longer leave him for more than a few minutes at a time. Visits to Fort Ruker were impossible now. Andy got upset whenever Timmy's name was mentioned. She thought perhaps if they got a divorce, Andy would improve. They could still remain friends.

Timmy's dream of a married life vanished. Feeling confused, he could not imagine himself without a wife to validate his male identity. Being married gave him confidence, filling out the image of a normal male, both to him and to others. This was particularly important to him because Tina could hide under the cloak of marriage, and no one would suspect his sexual identity problem. His pride would be intact.

Reluctantly, he told Peggy to proceed. Since they had never lived together, and never consummated the marriage, the divorce was granted one year from the date of their marriage. Timmy informed Darlene only after the final papers arrived.

"Timmy, you know what that means? You can marry me now if you want to!"

"But..."

"There's nothing stopping you now. Your wife's gone."

"But we don't really know each other, Darlene. And besides, you're just a kid."

"We get along real good, Timmy. You know it, and I'm no kid. I'm seventeen now! Come on, Timmy. Please?"

She was right; they did get along well. She was fun to be with and made very few demands on him. The male in him felt comfortable with her, and she was old enough to be married. The thought helped to ease his tension. He would be alone less. It began to look like a good idea. Again, someone wanted him.

"Okay." Timmy grinned. "You'll be my wife."

Her parents seemed almost relieved at the news. With their blessings, Darlene and Timmy were married on June 30, 1953.

Their wedding night was a disaster. Unlike Peggy, Darlene knew what she wanted and was determined to get it. It did no good that Timmy kept telling her he was tired and not up to having sex. She let him use his mouth, which she said she liked, but she wanted him inside her.

Darlene was so sexually aggressive that it altered the image in Timmy's mind, and he fantasized that Tina was being made love to by a woman. As Tina's identity assumed control, his male body responded. He achieved a weak erection, and with her straddling him, he positioned himself underneath. Darlene forced him inside her, and he had an orgasm for the first time in his life. The sensation was strange, unpleasant, and the fluid disgusted him. There was also a role reversal. Timmy felt as though he did not have a penis. It could have been Darlene's penis for all he knew. He thought to himself, *Did I screw her or did she screw me?*

"What the hell is the matter with you?" Darlene snapped.

Exhausted and revulsed by what had happened, Timmy answered with anger. "Well, you wanted to marry me," he said. "We should have gotten to know each other better first, but you were in such a hurry you wouldn't wait."

"No wonder that damned Peggy wanted a divorce!" She sat upright, nude, beside him.

"That had nothing to do with it!" He jumped out of bed. The sight of his own body revolted him, and he hurried to put on pajamas. In confused and angry exasperation, he shouted at Darlene, "And stop cussing! I hate to hear women cuss!"

"I'll do whatever I damn well please," she answered. "I didn't know you couldn't get a real erection, or I never would have married you!"

"All right," Timmy said, rage hot in him. "I'll get an annulment. Then you can find somebody else to sleep with."

Darlene blinked, and seemed to back off. "I don't..." She pulled up the sheet to cover her body. "Timmy," she said in a little girl's voice, "I'm sorry. I know I got a nasty mouth. I'm really sorry. I want to stay with you. Please let me."

Timmy looked at her. In a momentary blur, he felt that Tina was looking at her. *Oh, God,* he thought, *what am I going to do?*

"Okay," he said. He would keep things as they were, and calm, for as long as he could. It seemed easier than trying to figure out what else to do.

Timmy went back to Fort Ruker the next day. He decided to re-enlist and requested an overseas assignment. That meant change, and any change was better than no movement at all. Anything to get away from Darlene.

"You'll get an allotment check for a hundred thirty-seven dollars every month, so you can go ahead and get your own apartment," he told Darlene. "Later on, maybe you can join me wherever I'm stationed, if you want to. If you don't, that's okay with me, too."

Darlene said nothing.

8
Let Me Out

Timmy was shipped off to Okinawa a few weeks later. One month after he landed, the armistice was signed; the Korean War was over. The men felt cheated out of a chance to fight, and morale was low. Most of them were reassigned. Timmy was sent to the Twenty-Second AntiAircraft Company in Kadema, Japan. And then things began happening very fast.

He discovered that guns fascinated him. He became eager to find out whatever he could about firearms, and he learned quickly. He became a sharpshooter, and before long he had learned everything he could be taught at the base. The captain of his company selected him to go to gunnery school in Heoshi, Japan. He found the instruction easy, and in his spare time he earned his high school equivalency diploma. At that time, he was promoted to sergeant. He finished gunnery school second highest in the class.

He returned to the Twenty-Second Artillery as gun commander and was moved up to staff sergeant. He was assigned to teach gunnery to fifty-men classes. That wasn't easy for him, but he knew it was a challenge he could master.

At the end of the first week of teaching, he received a letter from Darlene. She was going to have a baby. Timmy was delighted. He not only was on his way up in the army, he now was going to be a father. He'd made it! He was accomplishing what a man was expected to do in a man's world defined by society!

But around this time he began having nightmares. They always involved Tina, and the same dream recurred almost every night: he would be standing in his uniform before a mirror. The reflection would blur and fade away slowly until there was no image. The terror of an empty mirror would cause him to scream. Then the image of Tina would appear with lovely, soft, wavy, brown hair falling to her shoulders, eyes large, brown, and compelling, her lips invitingly full. In his dream, Tina pleaded, *Timmy, I'm very frustrated. When are you going to let me out? You know who the real you is. You're me. You know I'm you. Don't forget. I won't let you forget*... He always awoke from the dream trembling and exhausted.

For days after the dream, the tension to dress as Tina increased. As weeks passed the dream kept recurring, fine lines appeared around Timmy's mouth, and he lost weight. He knew something was terribly wrong. There were moments when he could not think clearly; *am I Timmy or Tina?* At times he actually felt like a woman wearing a man's army uniform.

He prayed that Darlene would not give birth to a boy. He was terrified that a male child would inherit his problem. No other human being should be forced to live with such torture, the relentless feeling of living inside the wrong body.

March 18, 1954, Darlene called from Valdosta, Georgia. "Timmy, we have a darling baby girl."

A girl! The relief was so great his body trembled.

Darlene had named the baby Noelle. Timmy liked that name. Darlene was well, and the baby was healthy. They would join him in Kadema when the baby was six months old. Timmy had a family now.

For the rest of the day, he had trouble paying attention to what he was doing. Images of a pretty little girl wearing delicate clothes passed through his mind. He imagined her in her crib, years later going to school and on dates. In his mind's eye he saw her smiling, happy, lovely, soft, feminine, and always beautifully dressed. He promised himself she would have everything he never had, that he would give her the love he had yearned for all his life. Noelle would lead the life that Tina was denied. *I'm a father*, he kept thinking, *I'm a father*, trying to convince himself that he really was a father.

That night, lying on his cot, he continued to have images of Noelle. He imagined holding his baby in his arms, touching her soft cheek with his own, seeing her tiny fingers wrapped around his thumb.

After falling asleep, he was awakened in terror from a dream in which he heard Tina's voice, distinct and clear, *Wouldn't it be nice to be a mother? I'd make her a good mother . . .*

Several days later, Timmy started getting shooting pains in his groin. They were so sharp and sudden they took his breath away. He tried ignoring them, but they got worse. He went to the base infirmary and told the doctor about the wire going into his groin in Korea.

"Did you know your testicle is undescended?" the doctor asked.

"Yes, sir."

"Did you get any treatment for it when you were young?"

"A doctor tied a rubber band around it and strapped it to my leg when I was fourteen, but it didn't change anything."

The doctor shook his head. "Well, sergeant, the testicle has to come out now. Your condition is not going to improve, so the sooner it's out the better."

Timmy agreed, and arrangements were made. He was flown to the army hospital in Yokahama to have his undescended right testicle removed. On April 28th at 6:00 A.M., he was taken into surgery. He did not regain consciousness until several days later.

"Hey, man," said the patient in the next bed, "how are you feeling?"

"Okay, I guess. Groggy. What happened?"

"I don't know, but you sure didn't look too good. You were all hooked up to tubes, bottles, and crazy-looking machines. They came and took you out of here two or three times in a big hurry. A couple of times, I thought you were dead."

Timmy asked the male nurses and the orderlies what happened. They responded that either they didn't know or the doctor would tell him. Before he was discharged ten days later, one of the doctors finally talked to him in his office. "Sergeant, we ran into some problems during surgery."

"Were they serious, sir?"

"Your heart stopped during surgery. We restored your heartbeat and thought we stabilized the situation. However, a short time later it stopped again after you were returned to the ward."

Alarmed, Timmy asked, "What's wrong with my heart?"

"Nothing that we could find."

"Then why did it stop, sir?"

The doctor ignored his question. "You were unconscious for a few days, and were delirious at times. You kept asking to have your penis and other testicle removed." Timmy immediately recalled his conversation at the geisha house in Japan, when Phil told him about eunuchs. "Who's Tina, sergeant? You kept talking to someone named Tina." The doctor looked intently at Timmy who remained silent. What should he say? What could he say? "The records show your wife's name is Darlene. I think you should see a psychiatrist or a neurologist, sergeant."

"Yes, sir," Timmy answered, but thought: *I'm not seeing*

a psychiatrist or neurologist. No one's going to know what's inside my head. They'd boot me out of the army, lock me up, and throw away the key. That's all I need, to tell an army doctor that a woman is trapped inside me.

He flew back to Kadema, and after a short recuperative leave returned to his duties as a gunnery instructor. But something was wrong. He felt irritable, and frequently had bad temper outbursts. He became increasingly moody and absent-minded. Teaching became very difficult; he often didn't remember the men's names, and he couldn't keep their attention. He wondered if his behavior could be a result of his heart stopping during surgery. The doctor said he could have sustained diffuse brain injury secondary to respiratory arrest with anoxia following surgery. He kept reading the doctor's comments on the slip of paper he was given. It was difficult to understand the terms. Eventually, he was ordered to report to the captain's office.

"Sergeant, I've been getting a lot of complaints about you from the men in your classes. They say you're abusive and demanding. What's happened to you?"

"I don't know, sir. I just don't feel right. I can't seem to get along with anybody since that operation. I feel like the men hate me."

"Well, sergeant, they do hate you. And you can't teach men who hate you. Whatever's bothering you, you better shape up."

Timmy was unable to shape up, and things only got worse. His mind would go blank in the middle of a sentence. He knew it had to be related to the incident during surgery. To compound the problem, Tina would fill his thoughts at those unexpected moments. His tension mounted. He felt tired most of the time. But the terrible nightmares of a few months before did not return, and he hoped that when Darlene and the baby came everything would be all right.

Shortly before their arrival, he rented a small five-room house about a half-mile from the base. He furnished it carefully, and arranged for a woman to help with the housework. He felt proud of the little home he fixed up. He could hardly wait for Darlene and the baby to arrive.

On October 1, Darlene and Noelle arrived in Kadema. Noelle was a beautiful baby; even at six months she clearly resembled Timmy. She was a happy baby who rarely cried and could easily be made to laugh. Timmy loved her at first sight. Darlene had changed; she no longer looked like the thin seventeen-year-old he had left back in the States. Her body had developed into the shapely curves of a young woman. Her well-groomed, jet-black hair framed an evenly tanned, attractive face.

But her appearance was all that had changed. Darlene didn't like the house. She complained it gave her too much work to do. She found the maid unreliable and untrustworthy. She also complained because the woman spoke English so poorly.

The house became dirty and disorganized. Darlene rarely cooked, and Timmy ate his meals from a can or prepared meals himself. Often he had to give the baby her supper as well. But he didn't mind taking care of the baby; during those moments he and Tina became one, and he felt at peace.

One night he was holding the baby after her feeding, and lovingly, gave her a strong hug. Darlene lashed out at him. "Will you stop hugging that baby? Why don't you give me some of those hugs?"

Timmy's face turned red, and he put the baby down. After the surgery he had lost whatever sex drive he had. He couldn't even conjure up an image of being Tina having sex. And since Darlene demanded that he go inside her, there was nothing he could do to satisfy her. "I try," he said. "You know I try."

"Try? What's that? I want a husband who can love me

like a man's supposed to love a woman."

"Darlene, I can't help it. I just can't do it. And you won't let me do anything else."

"Hugs and kisses!" She blurted out. "There's something the matter with you. You better go see a doctor."

"I told you my heart stopped during surgery, and I've had problems ever since!" He tried to explain.

"How am I supposed to survive in this godforsaken place in the middle of nowhere, when you're all I've got? Well, I'm going to see about keeping myself plenty busy from now on. You wait and see."

Darlene was true to her word. She went out, leaving the baby in the housekeeper's care during the day and with Timmy in the evenings. She saw a lot of the other men's wives, and occasionally dated enlisted men. She went to every social function at the base, whether he went with her or not.

Timmy was aware of the gossip and that people were laughing at him, but he just didn't care. As long as Darlene was busy she left him alone, and he needed whatever peace he could get. He loved the baby; he didn't want to lose her. Aside from that, his life seemed to be falling apart. The dream of being married with a home and a family was disintegrating again.

He realized that Darlene had serious emotional problems. She was demanding, sullen, and rebellious. She wanted to be with the "fast" crowd and was promiscuous. Her relationships with both men and women were stormy and full of passion. She craved excitement. She did nothing but complain, and even if he could, he felt no one would be able to satisfy her, sex or no sex. He didn't like the kind of person she was and regretted that she was the mother of his child.

The need for Tina to emerge grew stronger, and to suppress the urge he had to make a conscious effort to behave more like a male. As the tension mounted his behavior as a teacher became erratic and unpredictable, and he showed such poor judgment that the commanding officer transferred him to another battery. Placed in charge of a gun crew, he had arguments almost every day with the other men. Then his eyes began to bother him; they teared and itched continuously. He went to the infirmary, read the eye chart, and was told nothing was the matter.

The next day, his new commanding officer called him to his office. "Turner," he said angrily, "the doctor says there's nothing wrong with your eyes. I hear nothing but gripes about you from the men. I think you're a goldbrick. I'd have your stripes if you weren't due to go back to the States soon."

"But, sir," Timmy said, "I had a good record before they operated on me. Something terrible has happened to me. I've worked hard. I suffered the injury in the service."

"That's all, sergeant. You're dismissed." The captain looked at him with contempt.

He was back in the States with Darlene and Noelle by December.

9
Exposed

Timmy's mother and stepfather had never met Darlene and Noelle. He knew they made a good-looking family and was eager to present that image to his parents for their approval.

On Christmas Eve, 1956, Timmy arrived in Gainesville with Darlene and Noelle. The excitement of seeing his family and surprising them with a wife and daughter was soon destroyed. R.L. was in bankruptcy; a new four-lane highway had taken customers away from the diner. Joe had been drafted and sent to Germany. Jimmy was gone, looking for a job. Timmy's mother had developed asthma and R.L. had high blood pressure and diabetes. The money Timmy sent from overseas had been used in attempts to save the business. Both his mother and R.L. were too absorbed in their own problems to do much more than say to Darlene and Noelle, "Nice to meet you." R.L. avoided Timmy. No one commented on Timmy's medals and ribbons.

Timmy was disappointed. Nothing he ever did turned out right. After a couple of days he left with Darlene and Noelle by train for Chicago. From there he would go to his next post at Camp La Grange just outside Cicero.

The cold Chicago winter was miserable; they didn't have the right clothing, and their Southern blood was unaccustomed to the frigid temperatures and gusty winds. They briefly lived in a motel room, while Timmy bought a second-hand car and rented a small apartment. He gave Darlene money he saved while in Kadema to buy appropriate clothing and necessities for the apartment. Then he left for the camp and reported to the commanding officer.

Only about one hundred soldiers were stationed at Camp La Grange. They made up an anti-aircraft battery with four ninety-millimeter guns. Through seniority, Timmy was made commander of one of the gun crews, bumping Sergeant West who had been promised the assignment.

For the next few months, driven by desperation to rescue something positive in his life, Timmy worked frantically and hard to improve his service record. He forced himself to memorize names, talked to no more people than he had to in case his mind went blank, and wrote little notes to help himself remember things. Gradually, things improved. He made few friends, but no enemies either that he was aware of. Sergeant West seemed to stay out of his way as much as possible.

Off base, with Darlene and Noelle in their cramped apartment, he found moments of relaxation and peace playing with Noelle. Darlene was sullen and silent, reading one magazine after another to pass the time. They shared the same bed, but they rarely touched each other. Once in a great while Darlene would ask him to use his mouth to satisfy her sexually. After her orgasm she would turn away from him in what seemed like anger.

As for Tina, she remained with him, always an important part of Timmy, and occasionally visible when he glanced in a mirror. The need to dress as a woman festered like an open wound that drained him of energy. His work at the post and his life at home made it impossible for him to satisfy that need.

At last, discipline and hard work seemed to be paying off, Timmy was promoted to sergeant, first class. But almost at the same time he learned that Camp La Grange was being closed, and he along with several others were to be transferred to Roseland just outside Chicago. Since he was required to live no farther than ten miles from the base, they would have to find another apartment.

Darlene was upset and resentful about the change and gave him no help. Affordable housing in the vicinity of the base was scarce. The best he could find was a one-room apartment in an old building. He paid the quarterly rent, and they moved in.

Darlene's resentment continued after the move. Soon it developed into a constant sulking anger. She rarely got out of bed. Magazines were strewn all over the floor. She neither cleaned nor cooked, and Noelle was left unattended until Timmy returned home from his shift. Only then was the studio bed made up, to be unmade a few hours later when they went to sleep for the night.

Timmy cooked, cleaned, and took care of Noelle. The more he did traditional women's work, the more confused he became. At the post he was Timmy, and at the apartment he behaved like Tina. He saw himself as a woman keeping house. He began wearing an apron with the excuse of keeping his pants clean, but in reality it eased the tension of wanting to wear women's clothes. When he played with Noelle or watched her as she slept, it was with the warm pride of a mother, not a father. When he held her in his arms, he felt the softness of Tina's breasts against Noelle's little body.

As he spent more and more time with Noelle, Darlene became increasingly jealous and sullen, becoming even less active than before. One night after Noelle had been put to bed, Timmy got a can of beer and Darlene poured herself a drink from a pint of bourbon. Timmy never drank much; Darlene had three glasses of bourbon while he was still nursing his first bottle of beer. Suddenly she muttered, "Shit."

"What did you say?" Timmy asked.

"I said, 'shit,'" she answered, and her voice rose. "Yes 'shit,' you bastard!"

"Darlene..."

"Oh shut up! You're driving me crazy, do you know that? This whole place is driving me crazy." Her voice got louder still.

"Darlene, Noelle's asleep!"

"I don't care if she's asleep! Why the hell should I? I'm married to a crazy creep who's a queer and have a damned kid to tie me down. Well, I can't take it any more. You hear? I'm going to get out of here!"

"Darlene, Darlene, shhh, please. Take it easy. I know it's tough on you. It's tough on me, too. Listen," he tried to calm her, "as soon as this tour is up, we'll leave here and go back to Alabama."

"And go from one shit hole to the other? Not on your life!"

"It'll be better, Darlene." He was frantic. "I'll get you a nice home. Things will get better, you'll see."

"Things can't get better with us, you bastard! You can't be a proper husband to me, and you know it! Prancing around here in a frilly apron like some dinky housewife and mothering your own daughter!" She stood up and knocked over the bourbon bottle. She shoved it to the floor. "Well, I'm getting the hell out of here. I'm going to take Noelle and go back down South."

"Darlene, you're drunk."

"Damned right, I'm drunk. What else should I be?" She sat down hard in the chair.

"Come on, Darlene, you'll feel better if you lie down. Come on, let me put you to bed."

"Don't touch me, creep! I'll go to bed myself."

She stood up, swaying slightly, and dropped her robe to

the floor. She opened the day bed with a loud bang, fell across the mattress, and a few minutes later was fast asleep.

Take Noelle! She couldn't take Noelle. She was all Timmy had, the only human being Timmy ever loved. Noelle was the only thing in his life that made the man and woman in him one, that brought Timmy and Tina together. Darlene couldn't take Noelle!

He put himself to bed, praying that Darlene would sleep off her drunken rage and forget everything she had said. The next morning, leaving her asleep, he dressed quietly and went to the base. When the day was over, he hurried back to the apartment.

"Darlene? Noelle!"

They were gone. He slumped in a chair, devastated. He stared at the unmade bed, the magazines on the floor, the empty baby bed, and the doll. He sobbed, then cried uncontrollably. He sat without moving until darkness fell and it was late. He rose, turned on a light, and took a can of beer from the refrigerator. He drank it fast, took another, and drank that. He sat down to drink his third beer, then got up to get a fourth...

A bottle on top of Darlene's bureau caught his attention. She hadn't taken her perfume. What else had she left behind? He walked over to the bureau and opened the drawers one at a time. She had left almost everything. Swiftly he opened the closet door. It was filled with clothes, women's clothes. Timmy's heart pounded. He took off his shirt and pants. Then he removed his underwear and was completely naked. With gentle hands, he slipped a pair of Darlene's silk panties up over his small hips, fastened her black garter belt around his waist, and pulled sheer stockings over his legs. Then he put on a half-slip and a brown-checked skirt. He pulled a soft pink sweater over his head and hung a string of pearls around his neck. Lastly he placed a ring on a finger of each hand.

Everything fit him perfectly.

He found her makeup and carefully put on lipstick, a touch of rouge, and mascara. He felt as he did when he first put on Sally's clothes back at the farm. The horrible pain within him began to ease. He saw Darlene's open-backed, high-heeled bedroom pumps and slipped into them. He looked into the mirror. Tina looked back at him. The torment of months stopped.

Timmy sat in a chair to think about the situation. His head felt clearer than it had in a long time. Although Darlene had taken Noelle, for the moment at least it was not an immediate priority. The naturalness and comfort of being Tina overtook his thinking about what had happened the previous evening. It was time to do something for Tina. *I know.* He recalled the men at the base talking about a gay bar in Cicero. *What was its name . . . Bernard's—that's it!*

He looked up the address in the phone book. Darlene had left a loose-fitting coat behind, and he put that on. Opening the door slowly, he peered out; the hall was empty. He walked quickly down the stairs and out to the car, relieved that no one was on the street. He drove to Cicero slowly, carefully, realizing that he could be arrested for impersonating a woman.

He found the bar. A faint orange neon sign in the window flickered "Bernard's." A dark curtain prevented anyone from seeing inside. Just inside the open door, a burly man in a black suit sat on a stool, monitoring those entering and exiting.

"Sorry, mi . . . Oh. Excuse me. Go right on in," he said.

Two rows of booths, lit by small shaded lamps, stretched around the room. The bar was located a few feet from the door, and a large jukebox sat at the opposite end of the room. Its heavy bass music filled the room, serving as background to the patrons' conversations.

Several young men stood with their backs against the bar, even though there were empty stools. They briefly glanced at Timmy when he came in, then resumed looking around the room. Groups of two or three men chatting with drinks in hands also noticed Timmy when he came in. Once he heard a shriek of loud laughter that sounded like a woman's, but he saw no woman anywhere in the room.

Timmy sat at the bar and ordered bourbon on the rocks. With shaking hands, he sipped his drink several times. Using the mirror behind the bar he watched the patrons, and when ever someone caught his eye he looked away quickly.

Most of the men in the room were young looking, not much older than Timmy. A few appeared to be in their thirties, and one man, obviously drunk, had the bald head and paunch of a fifty-year-old. They were all well dressed. Timmy noticed that none wore glasses, except for a tall young man with a monocle. He caught Timmy looking at him, and Timmy immediately dropped his gaze. He didn't have the vaguest idea what to do. He was about to signal the bartender for another drink when he noticed someone slide onto the stool next to him.

"Hi, babe." The voice belonged to a slender brown-eyed man of about twenty-five. "Let me buy you a drink."

Timmy said nothing, fearing that his husky voice would give him away as male.

"What are you drinking? Scotch?"

"No," said Timmy softly. "Bourbon."

The man smiled. "Aha! So you can talk! Bartender..." He ordered the drinks. "My name's Ned," he said. "What's yours?"

"Tina."

Timmy's voice became softer still. He was so tense and frightened that it didn't occur to him that this was the first time that he had ever appeared in public as Tina.

"I can hardly hear you," Ned said, moving closer. Their drinks came. "Well, here's to you, Tina." He took a swallow of his beer and put the glass down. "You new? I never saw you here before."

"Yes. This is my first visit."

Ned heard the accent and grinned. "Oh, a Southerner, huh?"

Timmy burst out. "Listen, my name's Timmy."

"No kidding!" Ned was laughing. "You could have fooled me. But then I said to myself, what's a good-looking straight female doing in this gay hangout?"

"You mean you really thought I was a woman?"

"Well..." Ned gave him a long look. "Of course, if I wanted a straight woman I'd be home with my wife."

"You're married?"

"Yeah. But I've got another little place near here. Nice place. Look, Timmy... or do you want me to call you Tina?"

"Tina."

"Tina. Look, want to come to my place for a drink?"

He was good looking and he had a nice smile. "Why... yes. I'd like that."

"Great." He paid the check, and they left the bar together. They had just started to walk toward the car.

"Oh my God!" Timmy exclaimed.

Two soldiers were coming down the street, Sergeant West and his buddy Corporal Travis.

Timmy's face turned white, and he ducked back into the bar. Ned came in after him. "Hey! What's the matter with you?"

The burly man on the stool said, "In or out, fellows—you can't stand here."

"Oh, wait—wait just a minute, please?" Timmy replied.

"What the hell is the matter?" Ned grabbed his arm.

"Those two soldiers... would you look outside and see

if they're gone? Don't let them see you checking them out!" Timmy pleaded.

"I told you two," the burly man was getting off his stool. "Please!"

Ned opened the door and looked out. He opened it all the way and looked to the right and left.

The burly man at the door put his hand on Timmy's shoulder. "Okay, out you go."

"They're gone," said Ned.

"Oh, thank God." Timmy breathed a deep sigh of relief. "I'm going," he said to the burly man.

Out on the sidewalk, Ned said, "What's going on? Are those soldiers after you?"

"No. I . . . I know them. I didn't want them to see me dressed like this. Look Ned, I'm sorry, but I really don't feel too good. I think I better go home."

Ned shrugged his shoulders and looked annoyed. "Well, I won't coax you," he said, and walked off.

Timmy took a quick look around and dashed for his car. When Timmy arrived at the apartment he noticed that the lights were on. "Damn, I must've forgotten to turn them off." He put the key in the lock and opened the door. Clothes lay over the backs of all the chairs. Darlene stood by the couch, packing her suitcase. She was looking at him.

"Jesus Christ!" she exclaimed, stunned by the sight of Timmy in female attire.

"Darlene . . . " He moved toward her.

She recoiled. "Don't you get near me." She stared at him, unmoving.

"Darlene, where's Noelle?"

She shook her head, still staring. "You're never going to see her again." She went to the suitcase, closed it, and carried it to the door. Timmy moved aside. "I never want to see you again. Jesus Christ. A freak." Her voice trembled. "If you ever get anywhere near me again, I'll tell Noelle and everybody else that you're a freak." She paused. "Oh my God." And she walked out the door.

Timmy sat down on the couch. He looked at the clothes left lying around the room, remembering the look of shock and disgust on Darlene's face. Sobbing, Timmy stayed where he was until he fell asleep.

10
Bigot's Trap

Timmy awoke the next morning. Darlene's clothes, now wrinkled, were sticking to his body. He showered, dressed in uniform, and then straightened up the room. With fear, anxiety, and grief, he drove to the base.

Almost immediately, he saw West and Travis standing with a group of men. West nudged the man standing next to him and said something Timmy couldn't hear. They all turned to face him and grinned. West put his hand on one hip and patted his hair.

"Good morning, sarge," he said in a falsetto. "How are you this morning?"

Timmy flushed. He passed them and walked on. *Oh my God, they spotted me dressed as Tina last night.*

Classes were already in progress. The men in his group grinned at him again and said nothing. Timmy tried to conduct the classroom lecture about guns.

"What'd he say?" asked West suddenly in a voice loud enough for all to hear.

"He said," a high-pitched voice answered, "that this here gun is some kind of real fancy stuff."

"Aw," said West, "what's a lady know about guns?"

Timmy snapped. He lunged at West, grabbed his shirt and punched him as hard as he could. "Hey!" shouted the other men who quickly separated Timmy and West.

A few minutes later Timmy found himself standing in

front of the CO's desk.

"What happened, Turner?"

"Sergeant West's been giving me a hard time all day, sir. I lost my temper and went after him."

"I know that soldier, Turner. West is a good man." The captain spoke firmly. "Sergeant, there are a lot of rumors going around here about you."

Here it comes, Timmy thought. "Well, sir, I've been under a lot of pressure since I was stationed here. My wife just left me, and . . . "

"Isn't there something else you should tell me, sergeant?" The CO looked keenly at him. It was obvious he knew that Timmy had been in a gay bar dressed as a woman.

"Sir, I . . . "

The captain waited.

"Sir, I've never been able to tell anyone this in my life."

"What is it, sergeant?"

"All my life I thought I should be a woman. I really believe I was born with the wrong body, and that there is a woman trapped within me."

"You what?"

"Yes, sir," said Timmy, frightened. "I know that sounds crazy. I look like a man, but inside my head I'm a woman."

"What kind of bullshit are you handing me?" the captain shouted. "How far will you go to prove you're not a queer? You must think I'm stupid!"

"No, sir. I'm not a queer, sir. I really think I should've been born a woman and something went wrong."

"Something went wrong, all right," the captain said. "I think I'm going to send you to the psycho ward."

The next day Timmy was sent to the Great Lakes Naval Hospital for observation. He was there for three weeks. For reasons unexplained, they put him in a ward for the criminally insane. Fortunately, the patients, not knowing what his problem was, sensed he was different from them and left him alone. Most of the time passed in a blur. He kept to himself, barely spoke to anyone, stared at the television set, and played solitaire. He saw a psychiatrist once, and told him that his heart stopped during surgery for injuries sustained in battle, and he hadn't been the same since. He also tried to tell the doctor about Tina, but the doctor avoided any discussion.

Timmy reported to his CO on his first day back. "Turner, I've got your medical records here. The psychiatrist says there's nothing wrong with you."

"Yes, sir."

"Therefore, I'm reducing you in rank for fighting while on duty."

"Yes, sir." There was nothing he could say. He saluted and left the office.

Out on the walk, he saw a wallet lying on the ground, and without thinking picked it up. He got into his car and drove back to the apartment, his mind whirling.

The next morning as he was dressing, he found the wallet in his pocket. *I should have turned this in right away!* he thought. *I'm not thinking straight.* He went through the papers until he found a name. It belonged to Corporal Travis, West's buddy. *God, why did it have to be his! Now what am I going to do?*

He found Travis shortly after arriving at the base.

"I got your wallet here," Timmy said. "I found it yesterday when I was leaving the base and forgot to turn it in. Okay?"

The corporal flipped through the wallet. "There's money missing."

"I swear I never took anything from your wallet!"

"Tell it to the captain," Travis said with contempt on his face. "My buddy saw you pick it up and he told the captain you took off with it."

"Oh, no!"

The soldier walked away, and Timmy went to the captain's office.

"I've been expecting you, corporal. I understand you stole a wallet."

"Stole?" He shook his head. "No, sir. I found it yesterday outside your office. I meant to turn it in, but . . . well, sir, I was so upset I absolutely forgot I had it. I swear that's what happened. I never stole anything in my life."

The captain got to his feet. His face was red. "Turner, you're a liar, a thief, and a homosexual. You're a rotten soldier and not fit for the service. I want you out of my command, and I'm busting you to PFC."

"Sir! Please give me a chance. I've told you the truth. I got a good record in Korea. I'm not homosexual. I think . . ."

"I'm going to give you a chance, Turner." The captain cut him off with hate and disgust in his voice. "You're going to get a military hearing. Then you'll get either a dishonorable discharge, or court-martial. And even if they should transfer you to another group, at least you'll be out of my hair."

"But, sir . . ."

"That's all, private."

Timmy waited out the three days before his military hearing staying in his apartment. He kept the terror and tension mounting within from breaking into total collapse by remaining dressed as Tina and keeping all his men's clothes out of sight. He ate almost nothing and slept little. The horror of those three days was brightened only by brief moments when he got a glimpse of Tina in the mirror or slipped into her clothes.

The day of his hearing arrived and Timmy drove to the base. He entered the room, his eyes black-rimmed and bleak, and snapped to attention.

"Private First Class Turner reporting as ordered."

Six officers, including his captain, sat at a large table in the middle of the room. They were large, vigorous men, and Timmy shivered slightly at the contempt in their eyes when they looked at him.

"Be seated, Private Turner," a colonel directed him. Timmy took the chair at the end of the table.

Each officer had an open folder on the table in front of him. It contained Timmy's service record and the charges against him. The colonel, the highest ranking officer in the room, was the first to speak. "Private Turner, you have been charged with misappropriation of money, assaulting another soldier without cause or reason, and with being a homosexual. Do you accept or deny these charges?"

"I deny all charges, sir. Isn't there an army lawyer here to represent me?"

Timmy's request for a lawyer was ignored. A major spoke next. "Did you assault a soldier in your class while demonstrating the use of a gun?"

"Yes, sir, I did."

"Why?"

"He was continually harassing me, sir. I finally lost my temper and went after him." Timmy's voice grew louder. "What I did was wrong, but he was constantly baiting me."

His commanding officer asked the next question. "Do you deny taking money from a corporal's wallet?"

"I deny it, yes, sir. I found the wallet. I should've turned it in right away, but I'd just been busted to corporal because of the fight and I forgot."

"You forgot?"

Timmy nodded. "Yes, sir. I returned it first thing the next morning, and I swear I did not take any money from that wallet."

"Are you trying to say, private," another officer asked, "that everyone was after you for no reason?"

"Yes, sir, I am. Sergeant West had it in for me because he would have been gun commander if I hadn't been assigned here. Corporal Travis is West's buddy. I think they planted the wallet so I'd get in trouble, and they lied that I took the money."

"I see," the captain said. He spoke slowly. "So you think everyone is after you and that the wallet was planted to get you in trouble. Tell me, private, weren't you locked up in the psycho ward not too long ago?"

"I was, sir." Timmy began to sweat. "But that was at your suggestion, sir. I had confided in you . . . "

"And tell these officers what you told me."

"But, sir."

"Tell them, private."

The room was quiet. Tension mounted. Timmy could feel sweat slide down the sides of his face. His hands trembled. Waves of fear rode through his body. He felt like vomiting.

"Obey the captain's order, private," the colonel said.

"I told you I was born the wrong sex. I told you I thought I should have been born a woman."

As though he had been waiting, a major spoke up. "Are you saying that you're a homosexual?"

"No, Major, I'm not a homosexual. I don't want to have sex with men. I'm saying . . . " His voice shook. "I'm saying that I should have been born a woman even though I have a man's body. Something in me, my brain, I don't know what to call it . . . but as long as I can remember I have always felt I had a female trapped inside me, in my brain."

The officers looked at each other. Finally one of them said, "So you're perverted, Private Turner?"

"I'm not perverted." Timmy was surprised at his own tone. "I think I'm different. I think something's wrong. My brain and my soul are female, but my body is male."

"I'll tell you what I think," his captain interrupted. "I think you're homosexual, and you're trying to cover it up with this crazy story of yours."

"Sir..."

The colonel cleared his throat. "Private Turner."

"Sir."

"Private Turner," the colonel continued, "I think it would be best for you and for the army if you took a 368 dishonorable discharge."

"But I haven't done anything wrong, sir. My record..."

The colonel went on as though Timmy hadn't spoken. "If you do, you understand that you'll lose all your G.I. benefits. But if you do not take this discharge, your rank will be reduced from private first class to private, and you'll be transferred elsewhere, out of the company. Your record will follow you. Things will not be easy for you."

Timmy bit his lip. Once word of the hearing got out, the other men would torment him. As a private, he would have to live in the barracks. There would be no relief from the men and no possible escape for him to dress as Tina. He felt devastated. Tears filled his eyes and he lowered his head.

"I have no choice. I'll take the dishonorable discharge, sir."

The colonel nodded. "That's all, Turner. You're dismissed."

Timmy rose from his chair and walked slowly to the door. He heard the captain's voice.

"Good riddance."

11
Who Am I?

On June 11, 1957, Timmy walked out of the Roseland Army Base with a dishonorable discharge in his pocket, civilian clothes on his back, and Tina's garments in a bag. After six years and four months, his army career was finished.

Alone, his pride shattered and his security gone, Timmy had nowhere to turn. He walked to the highway and started to hitch rides. He didn't care where he went, and the journey followed no particular pattern. He must have covered a thousand miles.

When his money ran out, he did odd jobs for cash and sometimes bartered for meals and a place to sleep. At night, when he could, he dressed as Tina. Several weeks passed this way, until almost without realizing it he found himself in Alabama. He made a decision to locate Noelle. The thought of seeing his daughter again and holding her warm small body in his arms helped him to relax.

But finding Noelle was no easy task. A ride to Ozark and a trip to where Darlene used to live yielded only an empty house with a "For Sale" sign on the lawn. He went to the diner that her parents had owned and found it had been repainted and renamed. The new owner told him he thought the family had moved to Valdosta, Georgia. Timmy hitched a ride there and found Darlene's father's name in the phone book. The small frame house was at the end of a run-down street littered with abandoned cars. Shaking his head, he walked on to the littered porch and knocked on the door. He expected Darlene's mother or father to answer. Instead, Darlene appeared. She wore a cheap print dress that was too large for her, and her black hair was cut short and unkempt.

His shock must have shown on his face. She straightened her dress and brushed her hair back with her hand before she spoke.

"What the hell are you doing here?"

"I want to see Noelle."

"You'll never see her again . . . not if I can help it."

"I'm her father," Timmy said, "and I'm still married to you. That gives me some rights."

"Well, I guess you don't know," she said.

"Know what?"

"We're divorced. You got no rights."

"What're you talking about?"

"The lawyer posted notice about our divorce three times in the newspaper. Nobody heard a peep out of you."

"But I never saw it. I was in the service."

"Well, I can't help that. We're divorced, and that's that. I got married again." Nervously she adjusted her hair. "We're staying here until my husband gets something good in the way of a job."

"Why didn't somebody try to contact me?"

"You were probably too busy getting dressed up all pretty like a woman to pay any attention to your mail," Darlene sneered.

Timmy's temper flared. "I want to see my daughter."

Darlene slapped him across the face. "You're a degenerate," she said. "If you ever bother me or Noelle I'll tell your high-falutin' family about you. You better forget about Noelle, you hear? She's never going to know about you if I can help it. I'm telling her you died in the service." She slammed the door in his face.

Angry, weary, and in despair, Timmy slowly walked away. He came upon a luncheonette, went in for a cup of coffee, and thought about what to do. It seemed there was nothing he could do. He didn't like where Noelle lived with Darlene, but Darlene was married to another man. If he pressed charges against Darlene, his cross-dressing behavior would surely become known to everyone, and he couldn't bear that. If Darlene's lawyer found out about his dishonorable discharge, he'd be finished. Anyhow, he had no money to hire a lawyer and he was not a Georgia resident. He couldn't go home to his family. He belonged nowhere, to no one.

Timmy thought about Chicago. His rent was paid there through the end of the month. His car was there. It was someplace to go. He paid for his coffee and headed for the highway once again.

In three days he was back in his apartment, looking for a job. He was hired as a dye setter for a plastic tile firm, but because the work was too strenuous for him, they switched him to a job as a custodian.

Living in the apartment was depressing. Everything about it reminded Timmy about his failures: Darlene, Noelle, and the army. At the end of the month, he moved to a small apartment in South Chicago. But his depression and loneliness did not let up. Working from early in the morning to closing time as a janitor was exhausting. He returned to his apartment's empty rooms, where his only solace was the radio and dressing as Tina.

When Tina was present he felt normal. He took great pleasure in dressing and applying the makeup he bought. Sometimes he found himself humming along with the music while wearing an apron and preparing supper. He would light candles for the table, keep flowers in the rooms, and occasionally buy wine for his dinner. Best of all, the Tina he saw in the mirror was vibrant and attractive.

After a while, even that was not enough. It had become a game and an act. He was still alone, and Tina needed contact with people.

Timmy knew there weren't many places where Tina could safely go. His voice, his beard, or worse, a trip to the men's room would reveal Tina as a man. But there was a place that Tina could go without fear, a gay bar. It was a compromise, because he wasn't a homosexual, and he hated the thought of sex with a man. Yet he couldn't think of any other option. He got the name and location of a gay bar on the South Side. Making Tina beautiful in his eyes, he went there one night.

The place was called Kinky's, but it wasn't much different from Bernard's. The same dark lighting, the same kind of jukebox, the same groups of handsome well-dressed young men standing, talking, and looking. But this time Timmy had more experience being Tina in this setting, so he was more composed. The patrons in the bar knew and accepted that there was a man's body under the women's clothes.

Tina left the bar with a man that first night. Just as easily, Tina left with a different man the next Saturday, and then the Saturday after that. Tina was liked and accepted, and no one ever used the name "Timmy." But the sex wasn't satisfying. In fact, it was horrible, and one young man named Damon made it plain that he knew it.

"It's no use," Damon said. "I like you, but you're not cut out for this kind of sex. You don't really enjoy it, do you?"

"No," Timmy replied, "I don't. But listen," he pleaded, afraid of losing even this much, "pretend I'm a woman. I really believe I am one. Maybe that would be better."

"But I'm gay," Damon answered. "I'm not interested in women."

"What am I going to do? If I'm not gay, and I can't have sex with women, then what am I?"

"Maybe you're a transvestite."

"Maybe I am. Where can I find transvestites? I've got to try to do something."

Damon told him about a bar on the far South Side called Diamonds. It was the preferred hangout for Chicago's transvestites.

Diamonds disappointed Timmy. The barroom was loud and cold, filled with men dressed as women. They looked and acted like males masquerading as females. While the outfits may have been beautiful, they resembled clumsy costumes on those wearing them. Timmy was also turned off by their behavior: feminine gestures and body posture were exaggerated, wrists too limp, and voices had a shrill, irritating pitch. Timmy thought the men who came to the bar for pick-ups were tough, older, loud, and coarse. This was a place of mockery, not femininity, and definitely not a place for Tina. Timmy couldn't masquerade as a female; in his mind he was a real female.

After two visits, he resumed lonely evenings at his apartment dressed as Tina.

12
To Kill the Urge

By June 1958, Timmy was convinced he had to move on. As though pulled by a magnet, he drove to Florida where his family still lived. R.L. and his mother had opened a luncheonette in the small town of Oak, but neither of them was there when he arrived. His brother, Jimmy, was behind the counter. He told Timmy that Joe was still stationed in Germany. Timmy visited briefly after Jimmy gave him the impression that he would not be welcome there. Sadly, Timmy went on his way headed to no place special.

He stopped over in Jacksonville and got a job as a short-order cook in a small restaurant. He rented a room in a cheap motel nearby. Timmy worked hard during the day and to the accompaniment of soft music from the radio became Tina each night.

At these times Timmy would recall his dream of growing up female, envisioning himself as a happy woman. He fondly remembered the early days on the farm, where he first discovered Tina.

The farm. Was it still there? What had happened to Granny and Uncle Harry? Were they still alive? No doubt his best and only friend, Rex, was long gone. These questions and memories impelled Timmy to ask for a day off from work.

He drove to Sand Hill and found the farm. Parked at the foot of the path, he could see that the property was weed-filled and neglected, the porch sagged on one side, and the cabin needed painting.

Someone came to the door to see who had driven up. It was Uncle Harry, looking much older and very tired. He recognized Timmy but didn't seem pleased to see him. Yet he didn't turn him away either. Uncle Harry told him Granny had died some years before, and he now lived alone. He said the farm was too much work for him now, and that he rented the land out back to a truck farmer. Most days, he worked at a gas station in nearby Clara. In fact, someone from the gas station had just called, and they needed him to come in right away.

Timmy offered to drive him to Clara, where by chance, Timmy saw Fred Reilly, one of Uncle Harry's grandsons. Timmy remembered Fred from the one-room schoolhouse. It was his father who was the school bus driver. Fred had grown into a well-dressed, self-assured young man. He invited Timmy to join him at lunch.

During lunch Timmy learned that Fred was a successful salesman for a national bakery company and had just been promoted to cover the East Coast territory. Timmy congratulated Fred and was impressed with his success and confidence. Fred seemed to enjoy talking to him. Fred asked Timmy if he would be interested in taking over his old route in Alabama and Mississippi. Timmy didn't have to consider the offer; he accepted. It was the chance for a new start that he'd been waiting for.

Timmy drove back to Jacksonville, collected his belongings, and returned to Clara, where he rented an apartment. He then took a three-day course in selling bakery products and began his life as a salesman.

Surprisingly, he found he was good at it, doubling the sales in his territory. He enjoyed meeting people, and he liked selling. Being on the road allowed him the privacy of motels, where in the evening Tina could reappear in peace again.

The year went by quickly. He began to feel more secure than even his best days in the army. He saw himself as successful and confident, on his way up, with money in the bank, and all the signs of a good life. He even bought a new car.

However, something was still missing and Timmy began to feel lonely again. His life was incomplete. He needed a wife, a family. He remembered what had happened with his marriages to both Peggy and Darlene, not to mention his daughter Noelle. *But,* he thought, *maybe now things would be different.*

On one of his trips to Silas, Alabama he met Carol Powell, a shorthaired blonde with deep blue eyes and a pretty face. She told him about her divorce, and her struggle to support her six-year-old daughter, Suzy. Timmy could see that she was lonely and worried about her financial situation. Carol seemed grateful for his company. Suzy liked him, and he began bringing her toys. Soon he was buying them food. Back on the road, he sent them postcards and small gifts. When he returned to Silas, he and Carol were married.

Carol's life had taught her to be cold and hard, and fortunately she was not sexually demanding on Timmy. Whatever Timmy managed to do sexually seemed enough for her sex needs. She was satisfied to remain alone in the small rented house while Timmy was on the road. When he would return home, Suzy was affectionate and playful toward him, and it thrilled Timmy to hear her call him "Daddy." She made him think of Noelle. Actually, he never stopped thinking about Noelle.

For a while, Timmy's home and job were secure and comforting, and his nights on the road, alone in motels, seemed enough for Tina. The picture was complete; the pieces of his life fit together. But Timmy's success as a salesman eventually changed. He was reassigned to another territory in Charlotte, North Carolina and told he had to live in Montgomery near the company headquarters.

Carol had been born and raised in Silas and was unhappy about leaving her hometown. Timmy understood, and in an attempt to make things easier for her he rented and furnished a large apartment. Then he bought himself a new car and gave Carol his old car. But after a few months, Carol became increasingly unhappy, and she and Suzy went back to Silas to live.

Timmy's marriage to Carol was important to him even though Carol was cold and aloof. He never had deep feelings for her, but he did care for Suzy. They gave his life a purpose and responsibility. With Carol and Suzy gone, he was alone in Montgomery. His free time became boring and unsettling, and he became withdrawn and depressed. Gradually the quality of his work declined, and with his salesman's charm gone sales dropped. The drain of sending money to Carol each week continued, and the bills accumulated. As his situation declined, the need to dress more often as Tina intensified. Dressing as Tina in the evenings was not enough anymore, as the urge to be Tina during the day grew progressively stronger.

One sleepless night, like so many others, Timmy got out of bed and paced the floor. He visualized that everything he had tried to accomplish in his life had failed: his family, the army, marriage, fatherhood, and now his good job. Every attempt to be a normal person had failed.

Suddenly he stopped pacing, and as if a light went on, he realized why his efforts had failed. He tried to live a normal life, but he was not like other people. He was not a normal human being by society's definition, and that was why all of his efforts to fit into the mold set up by society failed. When he told himself that, he knew he had arrived at the truth. Other human beings didn't feel like another person lived inside their body. They didn't feel like their bodies belonged to someone else of the opposite sex. No males lived thinking they were female, feeling content and peaceful only when their maleness was hidden under women's clothing. Clothes... women's clothes... Tina only fully emerged when he dressed in women's clothes.

The next morning, Timmy went shopping and returned carrying a long bulky package under his arm. He emptied the suitcase where he stored Tina's clothes and dumped them into the incinerator chute in the hallway. He went back to his apartment and unwrapped the package that contained a shotgun. He sat down in a chair, pointed the muzzle toward his face, and placed his hand on the trigger. Tina was in his brain, and he had to shoot his brains out.

Then he noticed the empty suitcase on the floor that had held Tina's clothes. He had forgotten Tina's high-heeled shoes that were on the floor nearby. *Wait a minute,* Timmy thought to himself, *if I couldn't wear high-heels I probably wouldn't want to dress like Tina. Maybe if I just shot off my toe...* Suddenly it seemed as if Tina tugged at his arm to stop him, but Timmy was determined to shoot off his toe.

"God forgive me," he said. "Either I stop living as Tina or give up my life." He swung the gun away from his face, pointed it at his foot, and pulled the trigger.

When Timmy regained consciousness the next day he was in a hospital. Carol came into focus, sitting in a chair beside the bed.

"Carol! What... what happened?"

"You shot off your left foot," she answered.

"My foot!!" He looked down at the large bandaged bulk near the end of the bed. Very clearly in his mind, he remembered Tina's pump lying next to the empty suitcase.

"Tell me," Carol said. "What happened?"

He felt too ashamed to tell her the truth. "I... I was

cleaning my rifle and it accidentally went off."

Carol gave him a hard look, and her face tightened. "Well, whatever happened, I'm not going to spend the rest of my life taking care of a cripple. This will mess up your job. Someone with only one foot will have a hard time getting work anywhere. I can't afford to stay with you. I'm getting a divorce." She walked out of the room.

Timmy felt Carol's leaving him was just another defeat in his life's long list of defeats and rejections. This one, at least, had not dragged on over months or years of torment. He did no more than sigh deeply, knowing that when the notice of her filing for divorce would come in the mail, he would not contest it.

By the time he was ready to be discharged from the hospital, Timmy had given up his apartment and lost his job. Since he was almost penniless and without a place to go, the hospital service department tried to find his mother. But she and R.L. had moved somewhere in New York and had left no forwarding address. The hospital staff did manage to notify his father, now living in Pensacola, Florida. His father came to the hospital, looking puffy-eyed and bad-tempered. "What the hell did you do to yourself?"

Timmy told his lie, "The gun went off accidentally when I was cleaning it."

"I didn't know you were that clumsy with a gun," his father said. "Now listen. I want you to know that the only reason I'm here is because my wife took the call from the hospital. She nagged me until I came. I live in a trailer with her and our two sons. You can come there, but I want you out as soon as you can get around on you own, you hear?"

Timmy agreed; since he was almost helpless, there wasn't much else he could do. His stepmother and half-brothers seemed like decent people. They took care of his needs in the cramped spaces of the trailer. His father rarely came home.

When he did, usually drunk, he repeatedly asked Timmy when he planned to leave.

As soon as he could get around on crutches, Timmy took a job as a short-order cook at a drive-in restaurant. He found a room in a motel and said goodbye to his father, stepmother, and half-brothers.

By this time he wore a prosthesis to replace his left foot. It looked very much like a wooden foot and allowed him to walk and stand almost normally, but with pain. His ankle often swelled, but he hoped that would go away in time.

Due to the years spent working in R.L.'s luncheonette, he was able to work efficiently as a short-order cook. The owner was impressed, and Timmy began getting small incremental raises. In a few months, Timmy had been assigned added responsibilities, and the owner offered him the job as manager. Timmy declined; he wasn't ready for that much responsibility just yet.

Despite not being able to wear high-heeled shoes, the compelling need to dress as Tina began to grow again. He first tried to ignore it, then attempted to cope with it, but it was no use. The tension grew so great that it began to influence his job. He was unable to concentrate and forgetful and became short-tempered with his boss. Timmy kept thinking he should have shot his brains out instead of his foot.

He finally succumbed to the pressure and bought some women's clothes, starting the familiar routine all over again: hard work during the day, dressing as Tina at night. At first he wore long robes to hide his prosthesis. Then he discovered women's boots; by wearing them, he could dress like other women. He didn't like living that way; it was incomplete and hidden. But he accepted it as being essential to his life if he had to keep living.

Eventually, Timmy and his boss got along better. His boss thought Timmy's tension was due to the shooting accident. Gradually, Timmy's workload and responsibilities grew, and so did his salary. He spent very little and saved a lot, and in a short period of time he had enough in the bank to open a restaurant of his own. Confident in his ability and experience, Timmy decided to make a fresh start in a new town. He returned to Mississippi and bought a restaurant in the town of Calhoun.

13
A Family Man

Calhoun, Mississippi was a small town consisting of a four-block main street with shops and stores on both sides. The surrounding countryside was mostly farmland, and in many ways Calhoun reminded Timmy of Sand Hill.

Timmy owned and operated a cozy family restaurant at a corner location on the main street. He served good and plentiful food, and the townspeople took a liking to him. Soon, there was a steady stream of customers. He opened early in the morning and, except for the dishwasher, was alone until Grace, the waitress, arrived around eleven-thirty. Timmy and the waitress worked together until closing time at ten o'clock. Grace got a ride to the restaurant each morning, and Timmy drove her home each night.

Grace Collins was a friendly, pretty, sixteen-year-old blue-eyed blonde, who was well-known and popular in Calhoun. She and Timmy worked as a team, and he eagerly looked forward to seeing her when she came to work each morning. Conversation with Grace was always pleasant, and the fifteen-minute drive alone with her each night became a special part of his day.

He was driving her home one night after an unusually hectic day, and they were laughing over some of the customers' antics when she suddenly said, "Hey, Timmy, you're a really special person."

"No...really I'm not," he said, surprised by her comment. "You're the one who's special. You're sweet, pretty, and popular. Everyone thinks you are special. Me . . . I'm nothing," he protested.

"Well, I think you're special."

When he stopped the car at her house and opened the door for her as he always did, she said, "Timmy, don't you want to kiss me good night?"

Not expecting the invitation, Timmy exclaimed, "You're just a kid! I'm almost old enough to be your father!"

She laughed. "I like older men. I never really had a father. He died when I was a baby."

Timmy gave her a fatherly kiss on the cheek, said good night and drove off, his mind in a whirl. *She really likes me!* he thought. *She's just a kid, but mature for her age. She's such a nice person; she seems so decent and kind. She's smart, and has a great personality. I like being with her, and we spend a lot of time together. Is it possible?* he wondered. *Is it really possible that someone so special—so lovely—really cares for me? Me, Timmy Turner?* His joy was tempered as he remembered the other women in his life. *I'm going to be very careful this time to not make a mess of our relationship or in any way hurt her.* This was the first time he ever had such positive feelings for anyone.

Over the next few weeks, they saw more of each other than before. On the day of the week that the restaurant was closed, Timmy and Grace dated regularly. They went to the movies, took long drives, and got to know each other very well.

Because Grace's father died when she was a baby, she had to work to help support her mother and herself as soon as she was old enough. She had many part-time jobs doing a variety of things from cleaning houses to operating the switchboard at the local hospital. When Grace turned sixteen, her mother moved to another town for a better-paying job, leaving Grace to live alone in a four-room rented house. Grace stayed because she wanted to graduate from her high school. She heard from her mother about once a month.

Grace was intelligent and a hardworking student. She skipped a grade in elementary school and graduated a year earlier than her classmates. Having completed her education, she accepted a full-time job in Timmy's restaurant.

In the course of daily conversations, Timmy shared with Grace the story of his life on the farm. He told her about his mother, R.L., and his brothers. He also told her about his time in the army, his marriages, and Noelle. He told the usual lie about his foot, which she accepted without question. She listened attentively and responded with sympathy, understanding, and tears in her eyes. He chose not to mention Tina. He was afraid to do so.

Timmy felt warmth and affection for Grace. He never had these feelings for anyone. She obviously liked him and perhaps even cared for him. Her face brightened whenever she saw him, *Could she be his soul mate?* But then, Tina was also a part of his brain and soul . . .

Grace's seventeenth birthday fell on a day when the restaurant was closed, and Timmy took her to dinner in another town to celebrate the occasion. Grace was in a jubilant mood that evening; she laughed and smiled more than usual, and looked prettier than he had ever seen her. Just everything about her was so special.

Timmy felt it would be unfair to lead Grace on in their relationship without her knowing about his problem of sometimes feeling he was really a woman. After much soul-searching Timmy decided he would tell her about Tina. *Could she accept the fact that he was born with a man's body, and had a brain wired like a woman, and that he had no sex drive?*

When he drove her home, Grace asked him in. As they sat at the table, cups of coffee in front of them, Timmy took a deep breath and began. "Grace, you know I care for you very much. Actually, I love you. For the first time in my life I really love someone, and it's you. But there's something I've got to tell you about me." He stood up and started to walk nervously around the room.

Grace became alarmed. "What is it, Timmy?"

"You think you know me, but you don't. Not really. I've got a serious problem."

"Oh, Timmy!"

"No, no, it's not that I'm sick. Honest I'm not."

"Then what is it?" Grace sat back to listen.

Timmy swallowed hard. "I feel that I'm two people. Not just one. And that's not all." He looked away from her. "Outside I'm male... but inside my brain I'm female. I have a man's body, but my brain is a woman's."

"You're kidding me, Timmy."

"No, I'm not kidding. I wish I were... this is serious. Grace, you see me as a man, and like I said, I have a man's body. But inside me, I guess my brain and soul, I experience myself and the world around me as if I were a woman. I don't know how else to explain it."

"Then are you telling me you're... you're a queer?" Grace asked, trying to digest what Timmy had said.

"No!" Timmy quickly responded, visibly shaken. "I am not a queer. I really think of myself as a woman. I can't help myself. For almost as long as I can remember, I've felt there was a female trapped inside me. She's the other me. I've even named her." He couldn't bear to look at her and put his hands over his face. "She's called Tina... I know that sounds crazy. Tina is a good, decent person. She's not a monster like in Dr. Jekyll and Mr. Hyde."

The revelation stunned Grace. She had never heard of such a thing, and sat speechless for several moments. Then she rose and put her arms around him. "Timmy," she said softly, "it's all right. Really, it is. I'll try to understand if she's part of you. Honest, I will. Please trust me." The compassion in her voice gave Timmy some relief from the anxiety he felt.

Timmy slowly pulled out of her arms. "That's not all. It gets worse. Sometimes I have to get dressed like a woman to be Tina. I can't help it. If I don't . . . " He didn't know how to explain. "If I don't, I get so tense I feel that I'll explode. It's the most horrible feeling. It defies description."

"Oh, dear Timmy. What a terrible secret you've had to live with all these years. I really feel your hurt, Timmy." Tears flowed down her cheeks. "I don't understand it, but I love you and that's all that matters," she said in a near whisper filled with empathy.

"But I'm thirty years old, and you're just seventeen."

"I'm old for my seventeen years. I had to grow up in a hurry being on my own with no one to love me or care for me. You are the first person I've met that I trust, and who has expressed feelings for me. Think of me as seventeen going on twenty-seven."

"Oh, God, I don't want to hurt you like I've hurt my other wives, and everyone else for that matter," Timmy said, biting his lip trying to control his tears.

Grace pleaded, "Timmy, what more do I have to say to convince you that I want to be with you no matter what? Your cross will also be my cross to bear."

"There's more," Timmy continued as he again stepped back from her, "I don't like sex. How can you want a man who's not interested in sex? Who doesn't even like the idea of sex? Who can't have sex? What about your needs? What kind of a life can I offer you?" he said in rapid succession.

"All I know is that I love you and want to be with you," Grace replied, attempting to soothe his frustration. "Your love is all that I want, with or without sex. My closest friends are becoming a nun and a priest. They are giving up sex because they love their God and church."

Within a week, Timmy and Grace were married in a local Presbyterian Church. They rented a modestly furnished three-room apartment above their restaurant.

Timmy worked long hours in the restaurant with Grace by his side. Grace made Timmy's life worthwhile. She enjoyed being his wife, taking care of Timmy, feeling his love, and keeping house. She did not press him sexually; they would lay in bed side by side with their arms around each other, and he would gently kiss Grace's face and hug her. At times he used his hands to gently caress her body. Grace never demanded anything more, and Timmy gradually grew more confident and comfortable in their relationship. At no time did she expect any more than he could give in their lovemaking.

Timmy resisted dressing as Tina for several weeks. Then he reached a point when he could no longer control the urge, and he reluctantly told Grace that Tina needed to emerge. Not knowing what to expect, Grace agreed and asked Timmy a few questions about how he wanted her to treat him as Tina, and said no more, although it was apparent she was apprehensive.

Filled with anxiety, Timmy went to the bedroom and changed into women's clothing. Frightened and not knowing what to expect from Grace, he walked into the room dressed as Tina.

Grace appeared nervous but managed to smile at him saying, "You look very nice." She was at a loss for words and fighting back tears. For the rest of the evening Grace tried to behave as though nothing unusual had happened, and as always she was loving and considerate. Timmy felt a great sense of relief and even happiness. To him, Grace was like a saint sent from heaven.

After Timmy removed the female clothing to go to bed he slipped on a female nightgown; he felt that he was still Tina.

Touching Grace, he identified with her, as if Grace were Tina being loved. Grace's responses became his responses, and as Tina he became fully aroused. It was as if Timmy had no male sex organs. Gently, he moved Grace on top of his body until she could straddle him. He went inside her. As her body and his began their movements, he never stopped watching her. He could feel what she felt. Grace and Tina were the same person. His arousal grew until he could control it no longer and had an orgasm, strongly, and fully inside her. The release and pleasure was so intense he cried out, "Oh my God... my God..."

"Timmy," Grace said later in his arms, "you haven't really got a sex problem."

He smiled. "Darling, you'll never know how much I love you." He could not bring himself to tell her that he imagined being Tina. It was so complicated that he didn't completely understand what was happening. The men in the army said they sometimes used fantasy when they had sex. Visual imagery wasn't that unusual.

Their relationship continued this way for a period of time. Grace never objected to Timmy dressing as Tina, and Timmy felt more and more comfortable about letting Tina emerge when Grace was present. Paradoxically, he felt easier about being Timmy now that some of his tension was relieved. Timmy and Tina almost became one, and they both loved Grace.

As long as Tina could be present, lovemaking with Grace became times of wonderful discovery for both of them. For the first time there was wholeness to Timmy's life. He was happily married to a beautiful and wonderful woman.

Several months later, two factories near Calhoun closed down. Since many of the employees in these factories were the restaurant's customers, business dropped off. At the same time the state was sliding into a recession, so people had less money to spend and could not afford to dine out. Eventually, there was no other choice but to close the restaurant.

"Don't worry," Timmy reassured Grace. "There's work up North, and I've never had trouble finding a job. Everything will be all right." And so they left Calhoun, where they had spent the happiest times in their lives.

They decided to move to Little Ferry, New Jersey because there was some light industry in the area, and rented a nice apartment in an old but respectable neighborhood. Timmy got a job as a drill press operator and was learning to be a welder at night. A few months later, he was promoted to a full-time welder position at a higher salary. Just as Timmy had predicted, everything seemed to be going all right.

Then one evening after Timmy returned home from work, he showered as usual and moved toward the bedroom closet that contained Tina's clothes.

"Timmy, don't," Grace said softly.

"What?" Timmy stood motionless with a puzzled expression.

"Please don't dress as Tina. I know you say you feel compelled to do so, and I've never said anything to you before. But don't you think maybe if you tried real hard you could stop dressing as Tina?"

"But I have tried. I've told you," he pleaded. "I don't do this for fun. I have to do it. I can't help it. You must understand, I can't help it!"

"I want us to have a good life," she said. "We just can't go on this way."

"Grace, what's the matter? What happened? Why did you change your mind? It never bothered you before." Timmy's voice quivered. "Grace . . . what has happened?"

Grace's cheeks flushed, and she lowered her voice. "I'm going to have a baby," she said, not knowing how Timmy would react.

"A baby!" Timmy replied in shock. He recovered, went to her, and held her in his arms. "That's wonderful!" His eyes filled with tears. "All right, Grace, I'll try, I'll really try. There will be no more Tina." He couldn't expect to be a father, to raise a family, and still use all those hours at night to be Tina, who continued to live within him. He certainly wanted Grace to have a healthy and happy pregnancy.

Timmy did try to suppress Tina. But as Grace's pregnancy became increasingly visible, the compulsion to dress as Tina grew stronger. He begged Grace to compromise, to allow Tina to emerge twice a week. Grace reluctantly agreed, but Timmy saw that it made her unhappy. Finally he forced himself to stop dressing as Tina. Grace noticed how difficult it was for Timmy to refrain from dressing as Tina, and she tried in every way possible to show him how much she appreciated his efforts.

Blythe Turner, a beautiful, well-developed, male infant, was born on July 29, 1964. By that time Timmy loved and trusted Grace more than he thought possible. He was extremely happy holding Blythe in his arms. There were times he recalled the days he spent with Noelle, his child with Darlene, who would be ten years old now. He wondered what she was like and where she lived, but he knew it was unlikely that his former wife would ever let him see their daughter. If only Grace could be Noelle's mother. The thought of Darlene as Noelle's mother made him shudder.

The more Timmy played with Blythe and held him against his body, the greater Tina's presence grew. Timmy finally shared his feelings with Grace. She listened sympathetically, and Timmy began spending a night or two each month in a motel so that he could dress as Tina and spare Grace seeing the transition into Tina. Grace knew what Timmy was doing on those evenings away from home. It was as if she could feel his pain. Instead of adding to Timmy's distress by sharing her unhappiness with his cross-dressing, she devoted all her energies to her baby.

And so life went on for them. Timmy worked, earned a decent wage, and was a loving and good husband to Grace, and a loving father to Blythe. At times when he was Tina, Timmy felt he was his son's mother and not his father. Two years later they had another son, Richard, who was also loved dearly and cared for by his parents. Like Blythe, Richard was a handsome, well-built, male baby.

To the rest of the world, Timmy's life looked normal and happy. When Timmy was with Grace and their children, it seemed to him to be a perfect world—as long as he knew Tina could be there at night.

They went to church services regularly, and Timmy became a deacon in their Presbyterian church, where his boys were baptized. He prayed very hard and often for God's help and salvation. But the gnawing feeling that he had a date with destiny was always present. Somehow he felt like the proverbial sacrificial lamb.

It was clear to Timmy that Tina never left him, and never would. The less attention he tried to pay to Tina for the sake of Grace and the boys, the more the stress and tension built in his body. He even unexpectedly caught glimpses of Tina in the mirror or saw her reflection in a window glass. Her presence was always there.

In late 1966, Timmy read Christine Jorgensen's autobiography, describing her surgical sex transition from male to female. He also read that clinics for those who had been born one sex and thought they were the other sex had opened at Johns Hopkins. Then he learned of a similar clinic at the University of Minnesota where estrogen hormones and psychotherapy were used in treatment. At last these individuals, referred to as transsexuals, were being surgically helped to become the sex that they believed was their true identity. Now

Timmy knew there were others like him. He was not alone. He was not crazy.

When Blythe was five years old, the factory where Timmy worked closed. He could not find another job in the state. Still thinking of the South as home, Timmy and his family moved to Montrose and rented a house. For about six months, he worked as a welder at a nearby shipyard that built nuclear submarines. He then got a job with the Alabama Gas Company. It was steady, well-paying work, and the job seemed secure. It wasn't long before he and a large part of the work force were laid off, and his best efforts to find another job were unsuccessful. Not knowing what else to do, Timmy called a friend from work in Little Ferry and learned that welders were needed again in that area. It seemed to be the best chance for employment at the time, so he approached Grace with the idea of going to work back in New Jersey. Grace agreed that Timmy should go, but that she and the boys would remain in Montrose, and that they could join him sometime later. "Moving around so much isn't good for the children, and there is no telling how long your job will last. We might wind up right back where we started. The boys and I will be here for you. You'll always have us waiting for you to return," she said as she gave him a hug.

Reluctantly, Timmy agreed and departed for New Jersey.

14
Pills for Change

Timmy returned to New Jersey, rented a furnished room, and again found work as a welder. A month later Grace wrote to tell him she had enrolled in a nurse education program, and proudly added that she had been awarded a full scholarship for the training. Grace said that the boys would be well cared for and supervised while she was in school. During the day they would be in school, and she made arrangements for them to be in an after-school program affiliated with the nursing school. Timmy agreed with the plans and was happy that Grace was continuing her education. In addition to his daytime job as a welder, he took a part-time job pumping gas at night to earn extra money. Whatever he managed to save he sent to Grace and the children. The fatigue from working two jobs did not provide Timmy with relief from Tina, her need to emerge persisted.

Timmy overheard the men at work talk about a gay bar in New York City; it had a reputation as a "wild place," a hangout for transvestites and transsexuals, as well as homosexuals. He was not particularly interested in going to a "wild place"; actually, the thought turned him off. He postponed going as long as he could, but the Tina in him succumbed to an overwhelming need to learn about and experience transsexuals, and he went into Manhattan one evening after work.

Club 82 was different from other gay bars he had frequented. The long, rectangular front room had a bar that stretched its entire length. Four bartenders took orders and prepared drinks at the standup bar packed three deep with patrons. The ceiling was covered with hammered tin, painted black, and the ceiling lights were dimmed. Posters of Broadway shows hung on bare brick walls. Because of little room to stand and the high noise level, Timmy pushed his way through to a back room.

The back room was a huge high-ceiling chamber lit by klieg lights attached to wooden beams. Dance music thumped from large speakers mounted on the walls. A rotating mirrored globe dramatically projected moving shards and dots of light over the dancing couples and the wooden dance floor in the center of the room. A rope encircled the dance space, separating the dancers from closely packed tables that filled the rest of the room.

Timmy found a table and sat back to take in the scene. Looking around the room, he spotted several men dressed as women. Their appearance and demeanor appeared gross to him, an image that would clash with Tina's senses of style and behavior. The exaggerated makeup and outlandish outfits would be offensive to Tina, who was always tastefully attired. One "woman" wearing a feather boa held a long rhinestone-studded cigarette holder. Timmy thought, *Tina would show more class*. He continued to look around noticing other women whose appearance was less garish, and he wondered about them, *were they "real," or could they be transsexuals?*

"Buy me a drink?" asked a woman approaching his table and smiling at him.

Timmy was puzzled. He saw her shapely body as that of a woman, but the wrist bones and hands were those of a man. A transsexual?

"Well?"

Timmy hesitated.

She sat down at the table. "My name is Marla. What's yours?"

"Timmy," he replied, continuing to admire her shapely figure and good taste in clothing. She wore a low-cut red silk blouse with gold threading, and a long black velvet skirt.

"Don't you have another name?"

"Yeah... Turner. Timmy Turner."

She made a face. "I don't mean a last name. My name is Mel outside, but I'm Marla here."

Timmy realized she knew his secret even though he was dressed as a male. "I also call myself Tina."

"Nice name. How come you're dressed like a man?"

"Well, I'm new here. I didn't know what to expect."

"You've got an accent. Where do you come from?"

"Alabama."

"I thought so. Pretty accent." Marla raised her arm to touch her hair, and Timmy saw soft skin, full breasts, and a smooth face. He felt a growing sense of curiosity.

"Did you come to New York to get hormones?"

"Hormones?" Timmy was startled, then recalled that Christine Jorgensen had taken hormones. "Oh yes, hormones," he replied attempting to cover up his ignorance about these drugs. "Do you know where to get them? I arrived in town just a few days ago, I figured I'd find out when I got here. Do you know how I can get some?"

"I sure do. Buy me that drink, and I'll tell you." She flashed him a bright smile.

A server brought Marla's drink to the table.

"You go to this doctor on Central Park West. His name is McArthur, Herbert McArthur. You don't need an appointment. Tell his nurse that Marla sent you. That's all it takes, sweetie, that and money."

"Thanks, Marla. Thanks a lot." Timmy stood up to leave.

"Don't thank me, darling. We've all got our problems. But they'll get you started. Good luck . . . Tina."

Timmy went to Dr. McArthur's office after work the next day. A nurse greeted him. "What can I do for you, honey?"

"Well, uh, I . . . Marla said to say she sent me. I'd like some hormones."

The nurse looked him up and down and nodded. "How much money do you have?"

He took out his wallet. "Twenty-five dollars and some change."

She nodded again. "Wait here," she went into another room, returning with two bottles. "Here's a hundred estrogen and a hundred progesterone. That'll be twenty-five dollars."

Handing her the money he asked, "How many do I take?"

"Bye, honey. See you next time," she said as she reached to answer the ringing phone.

Timmy decided he'd have to figure it out for himself and left.

The pills were supposed to start his body on its change from Timmy to Tina. He took one of each immediately. The next day he took three, and later that evening, while working at the gas station, he became so ill he could barely stand. His head pounded with a severe headache, and he became extremely nauseated, forcing him to leave early. On the way home he struggled to keep from passing out.

The next morning, Timmy was still too sick to go to work. Feeling better later in the day, he went to the library to learn about his pills. The librarian directed him to *The Physician's Desk Reference*, a resource book about medications for physicians. From the product descriptions for estrogen and progesterone, he learned that only one of each should be taken daily. In another medical book, he discovered that estrogen would not only enlarge his breasts, but also widen his hips and shrink his penis. There it was! He could acquire the body of a female and finally become one complete person! He went home with excitement and hope for the future.

Every three months the same nurse, who had come to recognize Timmy, provided him pills without question. He had been taking the pills for almost a year and had never seen the doctor.

When Timmy was laid off from work he returned to Montrose. He took three hundred pills with him, which he hid from Grace.

Grace had graduated and was employed full time as a nurse. Since Timmy had trouble finding a job, she suggested he take courses to be a beautician. "Then you could work with women's hair, which should please you."

He agreed and felt good about her being so thoughtful. He believed she proposed the idea to appeal to Tina. Timmy went to beautician school five days a week for eight months, learning about hair styling, makeup techniques, and other skills that a beautician, and Tina, needed to know.

Timmy had been taking two pills daily for more than a year and now began to feel and see changes in his body. His chest was slowly forming breasts. His hips were gradually widening. It was as if the woman trapped inside him was finally receiving the nourishment she needed to emerge from within his body. He was also relieved because the change was happening so slowly that Grace did not seem to notice.

As Timmy's body changed, the need to dress as Tina grew stronger. He was determined to not let his sons see him as Tina. He also did not want to upset Grace. She seemed content with things as they were. Timmy and Grace slept in separate beds and hadn't made love in months, which suited him.

Grace accommodated the situation with Timmy dressing as Tina. He had no wish to disturb the balance she had struck for herself. The situation was acceptable to Timmy, allowing him to have a wonderful and understanding wife and children, and the semblance of a traditional family structure.

Timmy finished beautician's school and received a license. In spite of his efforts, he could not get a full-time job, but did find part-time work at a beauty salon, serving customers who came in without an appointment. He also considered cutting hair out of his house, but gave up the idea. Instead, he decided to return once more to Little Ferry, New Jersey and leave Grace and the children behind until he found full-time employment.

The move back to New Jersey provided temporary resolution to the inner conflict that plagued him. He felt a strong sense of responsibility as a husband to Grace and as a father to his children whom he loved dearly. But he was all too aware of his uncontrollable need to become Tina, who could be neither a husband nor a father. Timmy struggled with this conflict until he realized that nature or destiny had made the choice for him. He had to become Tina. Away from his family and alone, he could continue with the change to a woman freely and with no harm to his family. He could let Tina emerge without constraint in the privacy of his room.

Timmy went back to work as a welder in Little Ferry. One day on the job, he suddenly felt an intense agonizing pain in his chest. Gasping for breath, he tried to stand up, but couldn't move. An alert co-worker noticed that something was wrong and quickly phoned for first aid assistance. Minutes later Timmy was on a stretcher in an ambulance on the way to the hospital.

Timmy remained in intensive care for two days before being moved to a private room. He was x-rayed, given an EKG and several other tests, and received injections to treat his medical condition. He was diagnosed with a pulmonary embolism, a blood clot in one lung. He learned that he could have died if treatment had been delayed.

Weak, but feeling better since his collapse at work, he listened to the doctor who sat by his bed. "Yours was a very serious, life-threatening emergency. The clot could have broken off and traveled to your heart or your brain. You'll be on medication for some time after you are discharged, and your primary doctor will have to watch you carefully."

"But why did it happen? I've been very healthy all my life," Timmy asked.

The doctor shrugged. "No one knows exactly why clots form, or why they break off. It's believed that certain kinds of diet may cause it. And certain kinds of drugs."

"Drugs?"

"Yes."

"Doctor..." Timmy hesitated. He had answered "no drugs" to a question on the form they had asked him to fill out earlier. "I have been taking some drugs..." he admitted.

"What kind? For what?"

"I'm... I'm a transsexual," Timmy said, obviously uncomfortable. "I've been taking female hormones, estrogen and progesterone."

The doctor looked at him intently. "Did you develop those breasts after you started taking them?"

Unconsciously, Timmy touched his breast. "Yes."

"Who's prescribing them for you?"

"Uh," Timmy said and shook his head, not knowing what to say.

"I see," the doctor said, his face stern. "Young man, you had better stop taking those hormones. Among other things, they increase the risk for heart attack, stroke, blood clots, breast cancer, and other medical problems. You may be killing yourself. You're better off leaving yourself the way

God made you." He left the room.

The way God made me? Timmy thought, *God made Tina, too.*

Three weeks later, he was discharged and went home with medication, instructions, and a warning to stop taking the hormones. But Timmy quickly found he could not hold Tina back, and resumed taking the hormones in spite of the doctor's warning.

Timmy recuperated at home for two weeks, continuing to take the hormone pills daily. His breasts continued to grow, his hips widened, and his skin softened like a woman's. Running his hands over his upper arms and thighs encouraged him that the hormones were producing the desired effect. He was finally becoming a woman.

When Timmy felt well enough to return to work, he discovered his male clothing no longer fit. In a bold step he decided to put on women's slacks and shirt, and with a mixture of defiance and fear he reported to work dressed as Tina.

Timmy was surprised and relieved when his boss remarked, "I don't give a damn what you look like or what you wear just as long as you keep doing your job."

There were a variety of reactions on the shop floor.

"Woo-ee!" shouted one of the men.

"Hi there, sweetie, give us a kiss," said another.

"Hey, Timmy, welcome back!" a third one said, punching Timmy's shoulder.

"Yeah, Timmy, good to see you," someone else spoke up.

"You sure been away long enough."

"How you doing, Timmy?"

Almost without exception and along with a few crude remarks, the men seemed glad he had returned. Timmy smiled with relief. They accepted him as he was. After that, he felt free to wear women's clothes at work.

As the weeks went by, Tina totally possessed his body and mind. It was Tina whose body he dressed, and Tina he saw in the mirror, as if Timmy had died when he had the embolism.

Meanwhile Timmy met several transsexuals on his visits to Dr. McArthur's office for hormones. He also heard about another club in New York City called the Gilded Grape. More confident as a woman now, he decided to go dressed as Tina.

The Gilded Grape was on the West Side of Manhattan, near the docks. Timmy entered a low-ceilinged room filled with mismatched tables and chairs and a long old-fashioned wooden bar. The lighting was poor, the major source being a few fluorescent fixtures on the walls. A conventional jukebox played continuously in the background.

Transsexuals in the room ranged in appearance from truck drivers in women's clothes to softly feminine females. Many were drunk. A few, smoking marijuana, appeared to be stoned into lethargy.

There were several straight-looking men in the bar. A few were flamboyantly dressed, others looked like construction workers just off their shift for the day. Later he learned that the straight men were either the transsexuals' pimps or were there for sex. He came back several times, hoping to meet someone he could talk to and learn more about transsexuals. He was not interested in sex. He would never be unfaithful to Grace.

One night, as Timmy sat at the bar sipping his beer, a tall, graceful brunette approached and took the stool next to him.

"Hi," she said, her voice deep and soft. "I'm Liz."

"I'm Tim...ah, Tina. Nice to meet you, Liz. Buy you a drink?"

"Yes. Thank you." She looked Timmy over carefully. "Haven't I seen you here before?"

"A couple of times."

"You really look good."

"I do?" Timmy had never been paid a compliment before when dressed as Tina. Pleased, he said, "You look wonderful."

"You're sweet." She sipped her drink.

Timmy scrutinized her intently. "You look familiar. Where have I seen you before?"

"Maybe..." she answered coyly.

"Won't you tell me where?"

"Maybe on television."

"You're an actress?"

"No," she shook her head. "You saw me on the news."

"How come?"

She sat up proudly. "My boyfriend robbed a bank for me so I could have the sex-change operation."

"That was your boyfriend?"

She nodded.

"You really had a sex-change operation?" Disbelief and excitement widened Timmy's eyes.

"Yes."

"Did you have to go out of the country?"

"No. There's a good doctor right here in New York who does sex conversion surgery."

"I...uh," he said. Timmy's hands started to shake. "Can I go to your doctor? What's his name?"

"Dr. Robert Grant. He's on Park Avenue."

Timmy felt a rush of excitement.

Liz smiled. "You're really just getting started, aren't you? Well, it'll be all right." She stood up. "I'm off to my boyfriend now. Take care."

Timmy stammered, "Good night," and left a moment later.

The next morning Timmy called Dr. Grant's office and made an appointment. He was surprised to see a short, balding man attired in a sport shirt and jacket. Dr. Grant was friendly and reassuring; he called Timmy "honey."

"What can I do for you, honey?"

"I want a sex-change operation," Timmy said flatly, trying to conceal his excitement.

"It costs four thousand dollars," the doctor replied just as flatly.

"Four thousand dollars!" Timmy's face paled.

"When you can afford it, we'll talk about it."

"What can I do in the meantime? I can't just stop trying to become a woman," Timmy pleaded.

Addressing Timmy's concern, Dr. Grant suggested he get electrolysis to remove facial hair, and injections in his cheeks to soften their appearance. He added that castration would do the most toward making Timmy look more feminine.

"My right testicle was removed when I was in the army."

"Then only one has to be removed. That procedure can be done right here in my office for three hundred dollars when you're ready."

Timmy made a series of appointments for the cheek injections. The castration would be performed as soon as he had the money. Back in Little Ferry, he used the phone book to select a nearby electrologist and called for an appointment. "I'm a transsexual," he explained nervously. "I'd like to have the hair on my face removed."

"Another transsexual comes here, too," said the electrologist.

Reassured, Timmy went for his first appointment. He was told the process would take a year, cost thirty dollars a session, and was painful. Before long he realized it would probably take longer than a year, and that it required several treatments before even some of his facial hair would be removed permanently. Nonetheless, he continued with the treatments, hoping for a smooth woman's face.

During one of his visits he met Vanessa, the other transsexual. She was tall, broad-shouldered, and wore her coppery red hair long. Her voice was fairly deep, but with skillfully applied makeup and attractive clothing, she certainly did not look like a man.

"When are you going to have your operation?" Vanessa asked.

"When I can afford it. It's a lot of money."

"Don't I know it!" Vanessa agreed. "I don't know when I'll be able to afford it either. But in the meantime I'm getting ready."

Timmy nodded.

"Oh, I don't mean the pills and things like that," Vanessa continued. "I'm going to counseling sessions at a clinic. They're for transsexuals who're planning to have a surgical sex change."

"I didn't know there was such a place."

"There certainly is. There are lots of us now. Didn't you know that?"

"No." He honestly didn't.

"It's right here in New Jersey. Would you like to come with me sometime?"

"I sure would!" Timmy's voice revealed excitement.

15
Becoming One

The following Friday evening, Timmy went with Vanessa to the clinic established by the New Jersey Medical School in Newark. He learned that the Gender Dysphoria Program started in 1974, and that its primary goal was to help transsexuals prepare for the sex-change operation through medical management, and also to provide some form of counseling.

It was there that Timmy learned that transsexualism was not officially identified and recognized until 1953, and that the first clinic for transsexuals was opened at the Johns Hopkins Medical Center in 1963. At that time, the entire field regarding sexual identity was still in its infancy. Little was known about transsexualism and its causes, though there were many theories. But despite limited funds, as much as possible was being done to help transsexuals.

Most of the patients at the Newark clinic were men who wanted to become women. There were a few women preparing for surgery to become men. The male-to-female transsexuals were given carefully prescribed doses of estrogen and progesterone; the female-to-male transsexuals received testosterone, the male hormone. Other medication was prescribed as needed, including tranquilizers and antidepressants.

The conversion surgery, as it was called, was performed outside of New Jersey, usually in New York. New Jersey and other states prohibited such surgery on the grounds of the mayhem statute—the deliberate maiming of the body to avoid service in the armed forces in the event of national need. The legal issues were still very unclear.

The topic at the first meeting Timmy attended was appropriate ways to style the hair. Since Timmy was a licensed hairdresser, he allowed his attention to wander and looked around the room. He cringed in embarrassment at some of the transsexuals present; their appearance and behavior were exaggerated, unrealistic, and phony. He thought that many of these transsexuals were there only to get the free tranquilizers and other drugs, and that others were merely transvestites who took the opportunity to dress safely as the opposite sex. He found out later that a few earned their livings as homosexual prostitutes and were routinely arrested.

After the meeting concluded, Timmy was interviewed and given a card to carry with him. It was an identification card, headed with the words "Gender Dysphoria Program," and went on to say: "This card acknowledges that Timothy Turner is a member of the Gender Dysphoria Program under medical supervision. The bearer has been psychologically approved to cross-dress and may be using a chosen name. In case of emergency call..." and gave the phone number and address of the clinic.

The meetings were held every other week, and Timmy went to as many of them as he could. He was asked to come to the clinic on other occasions for interviews that involved various physical and psychological tests. He learned months later that the clinic staff considered him a true transsexual; the more they studied him, the more convinced they became that he was genuinely outwardly male and inwardly female.

After all those years, Timmy finally realized that he was neither insane nor a freak; others had believed that and had told him so, and now he had found people like himself who wanted the same thing he did—to free the person of the opposite sex who remained trapped inside them—and were taking the steps to make it happen.

<u>March 8, 1976:</u> Timmy had accumulated enough money for the beginning step of his conversion surgery.

His first phone call was to Grace. He had not seen her or the children for a year and a half, but he had maintained frequent telephone contact with them during the week. He still loved them very much and always would, but there was no changing the way things were, and there was no turning back.

Timmy told Grace to start divorce proceedings. Over her protests, tears streaming down his face, he said, "I love you and the boys, too. You know I do. I tried to be a male and act like a man, but my mind is female. Please understand. Now my body is changing. I don't even look like a man anymore. It wouldn't be right for me to live with you and the children the way I am now. Grace, I have no choice. I never had a choice. Forgive me. You've got to get a divorce for your sake and that of the children."

His second phone call was to Dr. Grant. "I'm ready to have my testicle removed," Timmy said firmly.

The appointment was for the next afternoon. Vanessa went with him. Timmy stripped, laid on the table, was shaved, draped, and strapped down.

"Look at me," the nurse said as Dr. Grant gave Timmy a local anesthetic in the groin. After waiting a few minutes, the doctor began the incision.

Searing hot agony shot through Timmy's body.

"Stop! I can feel the knife!"

"It's only pressure you feel," Dr. Grant responded in a matter-of-fact tone.

But it wasn't only pressure. The pain was unbearable. By the time the anesthetic took complete hold, Timmy was bathed in sweat.

Timmy rested for a few minutes in another room after the doctor had finished, and then Vanessa drove him home. In a short while the pain returned. Dr. Grant had not given him or prescribed medication for pain relief. Vanessa took him to a local hospital, where he was given some pills to take. The pain persisted for several days.

July 23, 1976: Timmy was dressing to meet Vanessa and go to the Gender Dysphoria Clinic when he felt intense pain and pressure in his chest, and shooting pains down his left arm. He sat down, breathed slowly, and the pain subsided. However, the pain returned quickly and became more intense when they arrived at the parking lot of the clinic.

"I can't make it," he gasped.

Vanessa almost carried him into the hospital and placed him in a chair. She ran for help. By the time she returned with a nurse, Timmy was unconscious. The diagnosis by the emergency room doctors: pulmonary embolism, coronary artery disease, and angina pectoris.

Timmy was extremely ill, but it was not only his illness that brought many doctors to his bedside. Alerted by the Gender Dysphoria Clinic, the staff at the hospital was intrigued by Timmy's case history, and the mixture of male and female identities now so obvious on his body. The record of his undescended testicle and the prior relative hairlessness of his body made them believe there were indeed problems with both his hormones and possibly his chromosomes in his sexual development as a male. They thought the transsexual operation might well be indicated in his case. However, there was concern about his heart condition, and the stress usually caused by surgery.

Before Timmy's release from the hospital, a doctor visited him.

"How do you feel?" he asked.

"Pretty bad," Timmy replied in a whisper.

"You're pretty sick right now. You'll feel better soon, but you'll have to watch yourself."

"I sure hope so." Timmy fell silent.

"How long have you been taking hormones?" the doctor asked after a pause.

"I started estrogen and progesterone in 1973. The clinic gave me Premarin last March."

"If you keep taking those hormones, you're going to wind up in the grave. You must have been told this before. Those hormones can cause more embolisms and other illnesses too. You've got to stop taking them," the doctor said firmly.

"I'd just as soon die." Timmy's eyes filled with tears. "I've got to become a woman." Weak and overwhelmed with emotion, he cried quietly for a few moments.

The doctor spoke softly to him. "Just because you stop the hormones doesn't mean you have to give up trying to become a woman."

Timmy stopped crying, and waited for the doctor to continue.

"We know about you from the Gender Dysphoria Clinic records, and they've done extensive tests on you here in the hospital. If the size of your breasts goes down when you're off the hormones, we'll contact your doctor in New York and see to it that you receive plastic surgery on both breasts to keep them full. And there are other things that can be done too."

Timmy promised the doctor not to take any more female hormones.

September 9, 1976: Timmy returned to the hospital and had augmentation mammoplasty. His breasts were made fuller by the surgical insertion of a silicone gel.

September 10, 1976: A rhinoplasty was performed. Timmy's nose was surgically shortened and made thinner.

November 5, 1976: Timmy underwent surgery to have

the tattoo removed from his right forearm, the tattoo that had made him "one of the guys" when he was in the army.

December 20, 1976: Timmy applied to the county court to have his name legally changed to Tina Turner.

January 5, 1977: The document arrived in the mail: "It is on this day...adjudged that Timothy Turner, Jr., be and hereby is authorized to assume the name of Tina Turner from and after January 1, 1977..."

March 10, 1977: The date set for conversion surgery.

16
You've Got to Help Me

The director of the Gender Dysphoria Program at the New Jersey Medical School wrote to the Social Security Administration on Timmy's behalf. The director informed them that Timmy would need financial benefits for medical treatments in addition to basic necessities. Medical records to support the request accompanied the letter, and Social Security approved a small stipend for Timmy and his family. They also referred Timmy to the New Jersey Division of Vocational Rehabilitation in Hackensack, New Jersey.

The Vocational Rehabilitation Center was staffed by twelve counselors, most of whom had master's degrees in disability rehabilitation, psychology, or education. The counselors were assigned to clients who had physical and or emotional problems, and needed to be rehabilitated for the workplace. Some clients were referred to state-approved consultants for further evaluation and recommendations. Timmy's counselor referred him to Dr. Natalee Greenfield, a state-approved clinical psychologist who was well known in the state.

Dr. Greenfield had been the Senior Clinical Research Psychologist at the New Jersey Diagnostic Center in Menlo Park, New Jersey. The Diagnostic Center was established in 1950 to study characteristics of sexual behavior, and to make recommendations to New Jersey Courts regarding sex offenders. Top physicians from around the world representing all branches of medicine and psychology gathered there to study special cases. In addition to Dr. Greenfield's private clinical practice, she also published books and scientific articles, sometimes using a pen name.

On January 5, 1977, the same day official notification was received that Timmy's name was legally changed to Tina, she had her first therapy session with Dr. Greenfield. Timmy was then officially recognized by the State of New Jersey as Tina, and from this point will be referred to in female gender.

At 5:45 P.M. on that brisk January afternoon, Tina Turner entered the office of Dr. Natalee S. Greenfield. Her office was on the first floor of a modern medical building in Teaneck, New Jersey. Teaneck, located across the Hudson River about half an hour travel from Times Square, had been known as an idyllic community, a model of small-town America, and the bedroom community of Wall Street.

The waiting room was empty. Tina looked around and noticed a small sign on the wood-paneled wall that read, "Doctor is in. Please be seated." A soft amber glow from table lamps warmed the room. Paintings of boats serenely floating on calm water decorated the walls. Contemporary music played softly in the background. The comfortable atmosphere of the room was soothing and helped to reduce the inner turmoil Tina felt. As she took off her coat, a man walked out of the consultation room, smiled at Tina and left.

Precisely at 6:00 P.M., the inner office door opened. "Ms. Turner?"

Tina nodded.

Smiling and extending her hand in greeting, the psychologist said, "I'm Dr. Greenfield, please come in."

Tina followed her into the consultation room, and at her suggestion sat in a black leather swivel chair. Dr. Greenfield sat facing Tina in a matching chair. Tina began the conversation.

"Listen, you've got to help me . . . I'm a transsexual," she said in a low tone with a distinct Southern drawl.

"I know. I've read the medical records you sent me," Dr. Greenfield replied while observing her new patient.

Tina was smartly dressed in female attire and had the unmistakable proportions and curves one normally associates with an attractive female body. Her voice was somewhat husky, but no more so than other women. Her mannerisms were effeminate, but did not appear affected or forced. She sat poised with her feet close together. The hem of her skirt touched the top of her high-heeled boots. She wore cosmetic makeup and a light blue eye shadow to make her brown eyes appear larger. Her wavy dark brown hair was attractively styled. Tina tried to conceal her nervousness, but to the therapist's trained eye she appeared uptight and somewhat depressed. Dr. Greenfield had no doubt that this patient was having problems regarding the sexual change and was experiencing considerable confusion and anxiety.

"Your counselor at the Division of Vocational Rehabilitation has requested a psychological evaluation to assist her in determining an appropriate course of action for your rehabilitation. I have reviewed the results of the psychological tests you took at the Gender Dysphoria Clinic, but we need an updated evaluation."

"I understand," Tina replied. "I was told that an evaluation was required for me to be sponsored for job training, and hopefully for psychotherapy with you."

"Would you like to tell me a little bit about yourself before we begin the evaluation?" Dr. Greenfield asked.

Tina hesitated. She was studying the therapist's face and how she sat with her legs casually crossed. After a moment Tina leaned forward and said, "For forty-four years I've lived a lie because I knew I was really a woman trapped in a man's body. I've lived with this agonizing, intolerable condition for as long as I can remember, and each year it gets worse. My former wife has been very understanding, but we both worry how it will affect our sons. I miss my sons terribly, but I can't let them see me as a woman. I tried so hard to be a man, but if I don't get dressed up every day as a woman I am a mess. It eats away at me. It's like being two people—one person outside and another person inside. It's scary because I have to take care of that other person. I don't want to be a woman . . . and then I do. It's crazy and scary. My appearance is changing; I can see it in the mirror. I can no longer control whether I will look like Timmy or Tina."

Dr. Greenfield listened as Tina recounted the medical history that the doctor had already reviewed. One of Tina's testicles was removed following an injury she suffered while on military duty in North Korea in 1953. In 1959 she blew off her left foot with a shotgun blast, and since then was frequently in pain from the prosthesis attached at her ankle. Decades later, in 1976, she took the first step in the sex conversion process by having the other testicle removed in a surgeon's office. To develop breasts she took estrogen and progesterone pills until she suffered an embolism and a heart attack. In a few months, the final sex conversion procedure, vaginal perineal reconstruction surgery, was scheduled to be performed in a New York City hospital.

Dr. Greenfield got up and sat behind her desk. "Thank you for sharing this information with me. I would like to hear more about it, but we must start the evaluation."

Tina nodded and settled back. The evaluation lasted about two and one-half hours. In her report to the DVR counselors, Dr. Greenfield wrote that Tina functioned well within the "Average" range of intelligence on most subtests and related tests. Tina's vocational interests were in fields involving clerical, artistic, and scientific areas. Emotionally, Tina was alert, in good possession of her memory, and able to concentrate on various discussed subjects. She spoke spontaneously and in a friendly manner. Tina's speech was coherent and relevant. Her affect was appropriate to expressed ideation. Control over emotionality appeared adequate. Test results indicated that Tina was depressed, but traumatic situations in her past could have contributed to her depression. She missed her sons and had some guilt about being away from them and her former wife. She was concerned about completing the sex change process and the effects it would have on her family and other relationships. There was no evidence of a major emotional disorder.

Minimal neurological problems were evident. Dr. Greenfield thought that they could have been caused during the surgery she had while in the army when her heart stopped due to a lack of oxygen to her brain. Gender identity was that of a female. Sponsorship for psychotherapy was recommended.

Tina's counselor at DVR reviewed Dr. Greenfield's report and told Tina that DVR would sponsor psychotherapy with Dr. Greenfield sometime in the future. A psychiatrist, whose office was next to Dr. Greenfield's in the medical building, agreed to medicate Tina with psychotropic medication, if needed. Another physician in the medical building, a diplomate in cardiology, also would be on call for Tina if necessary. Actual job training for Tina would be postponed until recovery from the conversion surgery scheduled for March 10th.

After meeting with her rehabilitation counselor, Tina phoned Dr. Greenfield for an appointment. "I really need to have therapy with you before my surgery on March 10th," Tina pleaded.

"You're aware that DVR has not approved sponsorship for therapy with me until after your surgery?"

"Yes, I know. I've saved some money to use for a rainy day, and I'll use it to pay for the sessions with you in the meantime."

Dr. Greenfield was concerned that payment for therapy

sessions might add to Tina's existing financial burdens and cause her more stress. "Let's discuss it when I see you. I have an opening on Wednesday at 6:15 P.M., on the 19th of this month if you can make it."

"Thank you so much, I'll be there."

Tina arrived promptly at 6:15 on the following Wednesday. She sat in a leather chair facing her therapist. During the session, Tina appeared to become more relaxed, as if experiencing some relief from her inner turmoil. Dr. Greenfield sensed Tina's reaction and felt confident they would have a productive therapeutic alliance.

"I never had therapy before. I did see a counselor at the Gender Dysphoria Clinic in a group setting. As you know from my medical history, I had surgery while in the army, and my heart stopped both on the operating table and in post-op recovery. The surgeon suggested I follow up and see a psychiatrist or neurologist because he was concerned that the disruption of oxygen to my brain might have caused some neurological impairments or damage. But I didn't want to see a psychiatrist. I didn't want him to find out I was a transsexual. You know, I didn't want it to be on my military record."

Dr. Greenfield nodded. "Did you experience any problems that may have resulted from that operation?"

"I'm not sure, but I started having problems relating to the soldiers I was instructing. I also became forgetful. I'd have to think about other problems. I know there were several."

"That's fine, you might want to make a note if you recall something that you want to discuss," Dr. Greenfield reassured her. Actually, Dr. Greenfield was concerned whether a neurological impairment caused by the lack of oxygen to her brain could have intensified any of Tina's emotional problems, but she sensed Tina had other things she wanted to discuss during the session.

Dr. Greenfield continued, "Since you never had psychotherapy before, let me explain what therapy is about. To start with, in therapy, the patient usually sets goals. When we last met, you said you wanted to get your body and mind together and have peace of mind."

Tina shook her head in agreement.

"Therapy is also about other changes. In your case, you are making a major change regarding your sexual identity by having conversion surgery. There might be other changes that you want to make... for example, a change in your occupation. You said that you wanted to have good relationships with people, and, last but not least, you said you wanted to improve the feelings and resolve conflicts you are experiencing that are upsetting to you."

"I want to deal with all those issues, but I have others I would like to discuss with you first. I have a lot of guilt about having to leave my sons and former wife. I can imagine the pain they must feel just as I did when my father left my mother and me. Of course, my father wasn't a transsexual so he didn't have problems like mine. He was an alcoholic and a womanizer, and he abused my mother and me until he left us. Despite his behavior, I wanted him to love me, to be proud of me, to want me. He acted like he was ashamed of me for being small and inadequate. He was so good-looking and strong. He seemed to blame my mother for having a sorry excuse for a son like me."

"Do you think that had anything to do with your wanting to be a girl?"

"No. It just made me more determined to make him proud of me as a boy. He didn't seem to like my brothers or little girls either. He just didn't like children."

"We'll come back to your relationship with your father at a later time. Is there anything else that you want to discuss in therapy today?"

Tina thought long and hard. "Well, I just don't know if

I'm going to survive the conversion surgery. I am concerned about God, religion, and death. Can you help me deal with that before March 10th?"

"We'll discuss that at our next session, Wednesday the 26th at 6:15 P.M." Dr. Greenfield handed Tina an appointment card.

The following week, Dr. Greenfield greeted Tina and began the session. "Last week you said you were concerned about God, religion, and death. Do you want to discuss those issues at this session?"

Tina nodded and began. "I always attended church every Sunday. My sons were baptized in the church where I had been a deacon for over six years. They also went to Sunday school there. I never blamed God for my problems, like some people do. Every day I pray to God to change my sex. I've been ripped apart searching for dignity and have tried to keep my sanity at the same time." She took a deep breath and continued, "It seems like just about everyone I know despises me because I'm different. It seems like if you're different, you're condemned for that reason alone."

"Who is everyone?"

"My family. My country. Society in general. Everyone, except my former wife. I've been rejected by my brothers. They won't let my mother have anything to do with me. I'm afraid to leave my apartment because kids taunt me and threaten to beat me up. And my country! After I earned five service ribbons I got thrown out of the army. They spotted me off post in a gay bar, framed me, and gave me a dishonorable discharge. How do you think it feels to be humiliated by all those people who consider themselves crusaders against anyone who has an identity problem with their sexuality?"

Dr. Greenfield remained silent. Tina was pouring her heart out.

"We are all prisoners, all of us . . . transsexuals, transvestites, and homosexuals. We are in the prison of our bodies and in the prison of a society that can't understand." Tina's eyes searched deep into the doctor's for some reaction.

To Dr. Greenfield, Tina emerged as an utterly unhappy person that society refused to understand or acknowledge. She realized that anti-sexual crusaders believe that people like Tina are no-good scoundrels who have no respect for their God-given bodies. Anita Bryant, who spearheaded a drive against people with gender identity problems, was quoted as saying, "If homosexuality were the normal way, God would have made Adam and Bruce." Dr. Greenfield thought, *What would people like Bryant say about transsexuals?*

"Could you tell me how the church and pastors feel on this subject?" Tina asked.

"What church do you attend?"

"The Presbyterian Church."

"Why don't you meet with your minister and share your concerns with him?"

"I'm embarrassed to meet with him since I've become Tina. I'm not ready for that yet."

"Well, moral aspects of the identity in sexuality differ among prominent theologians. There's an expression that if you see twelve doctors you might get twelve different diagnoses and recommendations for the presenting problem. The same would probably be true among the clergy of different faiths regarding their views on the moral aspects of conversion surgery for the transsexual."

"I can understand that. Can you tell me a little bit more about it?" Tina reflected on the comments and waited for Dr. Greenfield to continue.

"I recall a Presbyterian minister stating that if conversion surgery could help transsexuals to lead a productive life there would be no moral objection on his part. Again, you really should talk to your minister.

"Over the years I have supervised many interns who were studying at universities to obtain a doctoral degree in psychology. Some of these interns were ministers and priests, and we often discussed the issues you raised. The bottom line is that if one believes in the immortality of the soul, and there is a conflict between the identity of the body and the soul, the body should yield. Of course, not all of them shared the same opinions."

"Do other psychologists share your opinion on this problem?" Tina asked.

"Again, you would probably get different reactions from different psychologists. Many psychologists belong to the American Psychological Association that is made up of about fifty-five divisions, including the Psychology of Religion. There also is a division for the Psychological Study of Lesbian, Gay, and Bisexual Issues."

"Really?" Tina exclaimed.

Tina continued therapy with Dr. Greenfield every Wednesday through March 9th. During the sessions they discussed subjects that concerned Tina and how she could cope with the changes she was about to encounter with her new sexual identity.

As Tina was leaving on March 9th, Dr. Greenfield said, "This was our last session before the operation. How do you feel?"

"Very excited and a little scared. I know I'm taking a chance with my heart condition. They told me I might die." She paused and raised her chin. "But I don't care! I've waited all my life for this. I'll die anyway if it doesn't happen. It's like if I wake up afterward, my nightmare will be over. I'll be a whole person for the first time."

17
Conversion Rebirth

On March 10, 1977, at 11:30 A.M., Tina was taken into surgery. Because of her heart condition, she had been given a spinal instead of a general anesthetic. She felt nothing during the operation and was only able to see the tops of the surgical team's bodies and their masked faces. Dr. Grant was indistinguishable from the others. In a semi-conscious state she was barely aware of their voices as the surgery progressed.

Two hours later, after Tina was brought to the recovery room, Dr. Grant came to her bedside. He was obviously pleased with the results of the surgery. "You're doing fine. The results are good enough to fool both gynecologists and lovers." Tina smiled weakly but gratefully and drifted into a deep sleep.

She remained hospitalized for six days, suffering considerable pain, but her great happiness made it bearable. On the fourth day, Dr. Grant removed the bandages. He cautioned her that the stitches wouldn't look pretty, and she would still be swollen from the surgery. However, she would be able to see the general shape of her female genitals. While the stitches and swelling looked unsightly, she could see what was there. Timmy's penis was gone. Tina had a female body.

On March 16th, Tina was discharged and taken home by ambulance. Alone in her apartment, she followed the doctor's instructions carefully. She took sitz baths at regular intervals.

The vaginal stent, the "dildo," had to be removed and replaced after each trip to the bathroom, a difficult and painful process. She had to learn how to urinate like a woman. While at first she lacked control, the process pleased her immensely. Every so often she would examine her vagina in a mirror. The sight of herself as a woman lifted her spirits and kept her smiling for hours afterward. At last, her body had no appearance of a male anatomy.

Dr. Greenfield called one morning. "How are you doing, Tina?"

"Okay, I guess, but..."

"What is it?"

"Well, I have very little food in the apartment, and I'm too weak to go shopping. I hurt when I sit, and I hurt when I stand."

"The hurt will go away in time. Isn't the pain already less than when you first left the hospital?"

"Yes, I suppose so."

"Why don't you have any food? Haven't any friends been over to visit you?"

"Friends?" There was sarcasm in Tina's voice. "What friends? My transsexual friends haven't come near me, and haven't called. They must be jealous."

"I see... if you wish, I'll be glad to food shop for you. Give me a list and directions to your apartment. I'll bring you whatever you need."

A few hours later Dr. Greenfield arrived at Tina's apartment. Looking around, she noted that the furnishings were sparse, but that the living space, consisting of a bedroom and a living room with a Pullman kitchen that was hidden behind a screen, had a warm, comfortable, and feminine appearance.

Dressed in a long silk robe, Tina remained in bed. Dr. Greenfield noticed that some earlier tension lines were gone from her face. She looked younger.

"Tina! You really look good!"

Tina smiled. "Thank you. I wish I felt good. I'm still feeling some pain."

Dr. Greenfield started unpacking and storing the groceries. "Here's the food. There's roast chicken, and soup, and enough canned and frozen food to keep you supplied for about a week. By then you should be feeling much stronger." Finishing, she sat down on a chair by the bed and they talked. Tina chatted away, sharing her feelings and her medical condition with Dr. Greenfield, especially the pain.

"I could help to relieve the pain. That is, if you want me to."

"Please, yes . . . that would be wonderful."

"Pain can be controlled through hypnosis. It is an effective procedure to use in certain instances. In fact, there are some surgeries where hypnosis is substituted for anesthesia."

"Please, let's do it," Tina said.

Dr. Greenfield put Tina into a hypnotic state and offered pain relief suggestions. Tina proved to be a good subject.

"I do feel better!" she exclaimed when brought out of hypnosis.

A week later, Tina was well enough to make the first of many visits to Dr. Grant in New York City for a post-operative checkup.

"You look wonderful, Tina," Dr. Grant said. "How do you feel?"

"I did hurt a lot. But Dr. Greenfield, my therapist, was able to reduce the pain through hypnosis."

The examination went well, and Tina drove from Manhattan to Dr. Greenfield's office for her scheduled appointment.

Tina discussed her visit to Dr. Grant. "He was pleased to

hear how you helped to reduce my pain using hypnosis."

"It's good to hear that you are doing so well physically," Dr. Greenfield said. "How do you feel otherwise?"

Tina sat back in her chair and smiled, as though she had been waiting for the question. "For the first time in my life, I'm really happy. I feel like one person. When I'm with people, I don't have to worry because I have nothing to hide. I don't have to pretend about anything. I'm really a woman now. It's a whole new world for me. But I don't understand why certain things still happen. Why do people have to hurt other people? When I went out of my apartment today, some children started to tease me. They told me I wasn't a lady, that their mothers had told them I was really a man. That hurt. And my landlady won't even talk to me anymore. I guess I'll have to move where no one knew me before."

Dr. Greenfield nodded. "That might be a good idea."

"I called Grace, my former wife, and told her about the operation. She said she'd like to see me, and how I look. Maybe it would be okay for her to see me, but I'm not ready to let my children see me now. Maybe later I'll go down there just to see them playing outdoors, without being seen. I miss them so much.

"And I do want to see my mother. Did I tell you I learned where she now lives? She's in New York City, Washington Heights. That's not far from where I live. I wrote her and told her about my surgery."

"You did?" Dr. Greenfield was surprised. Tina was certainly wasting no time trying to re-establish contact with her family.

Tina continued. "Maybe my mother will care for me as a daughter since she never cared for me as her son. When I feel better, I'll go to her apartment to let her see me.

"Changing the subject," Tina said, "I would like to become a medical secretary. Maybe I could get a job in a hospital. Wouldn't it be something if my surgeon hired me to work for him? Do you think I could start school as soon as I'm stronger?"

Dr. Greenfield could see that Tina was definitely feeling better about herself. "Tina, since you haven't started school and aren't working, this might be a good time to write your life story, starting when you were a child from as early as you can remember. Then we can refer to it during our therapy sessions."

"That's a great idea," Tina responded, "but what if I have a problem recalling things in my past?"

"Well then we'll do age regression through hypnosis," Dr. Greenfield said. "You seem to respond well to hypnosis."

Tina was enthusiastic. "I'll starting writing my life story right away! Maybe you can use it in writing a book about me?"

"Maybe, but let's wait and see."

"Oh, I almost forgot, I'm going back to the hospital in New Jersey next month. They're giving a seminar on transsexualism for the doctors and nurses, and they asked me if I'd come and answer some questions. They're even going to tape it." Tina smiled. "Can you imagine? Doctors and nurses actually wanting to ask me questions!"

A few weeks later, Tina went to the Gender Dysphoria Clinic in Newark. Someone was to meet her at the third-floor elevator and escort her to the seminar room.

"Excuse me," a young nurse said as Tina approached. "Did you notice anyone downstairs who seemed to be waiting?"

"No, I didn't."

The nurse looked at her watch. "I'm supposed to meet someone here at two, and it's after that now."

"Is this someone's name Turner?"

"As a matter of fact, it is," said the nurse. "How did you know?"

"My name's Turner. Tina Turner."

The nurse flushed. "Oh! I'm sorry. I'd never have known you were a man. Oh! I mean you look like a real woman. Oh, dear." She stopped. "You're really an attractive-looking woman."

Tina smiled. "Thank you."

They entered a darkened conference room where a doctor was narrating a film on the conversion surgery from male to female. "... he's creating a pocket in the muscle tissue between the urethra, bladder, and anterior rectal wall by blunt and sharp dissection..." Tina avoided watching the procedure. It was too painful and upsetting to see.

The lights went on. "I see our guest has arrived. This is Tina Turner. She had this procedure performed about a month ago and has graciously agreed to answer any questions you might have."

"Miss Turner." It was the first time she had been called that. "Miss Turner," a young doctor asked, "how old are you?"

"Forty-four."

"Isn't that a little old for sex-change surgery?"

"I couldn't afford it before!"

The doctors laughed.

"How much did it cost?"

"All the hospitalizations and other surgery probably cost me close to ten thousand dollars. And that doesn't include drugs, or electrolysis, which is still costing me about one-twenty a month."

"Why did you undergo surgery?" another doctor asked. "Couldn't you be satisfied with just dressing as a female?"

"No," Tina said. "Real transsexuals want their bodies to match the sex they feel they are within themselves, even if that means surgery. Transvestites are different. They don't want to change their sex. It's enough for them to dress like the opposite sex once in a while."

"Aren't you really a homosexual?" asked another doctor.

"No, I'm not. As you know, homosexuality is when two people of the same gender are sexually attracted to each other. I never really thought of myself as a man, and I never really would like letting another man have sex with me. I guess that does sound a little confusing," she added at the sound of someone's murmur.

"Were you ever married?" a nurse asked.

"Yes, and I have three children."

"Do you ever have second thoughts about what you've done?"

"Never. It was impossible for me to keep on living as a man. I had no choice. I'm sad that I can't see my children and former wife, but above all, I don't want to hurt them. Right now I want them to remember me as their father. This would be very hard for them to understand, and I don't want them to be ashamed of me for being my children. Maybe someday when they are old enough to understand they will be told."

"How old were you when you first realized you were a transsexual?" someone else asked.

"I didn't know anything about transsexualism until I read Christine Jorgensen's book in the late sixties. I was about thirty-four. But ever since I was very young, maybe four or five, I thought of myself as being a girl. I believed a little girl was trapped inside my body and she had to come out. I thought I was the only one in the world who felt that way. It wasn't until I read about Christine Jorgensen that I realized there were other people like me."

"What do you think gives you the right to call yourself a woman?" a deep-voiced doctor asked.

"I don't call myself a woman," Tina answered. "Legally I am a woman."

As if sensing her anger and hurt at the question, the moderator of the seminar spoke up. "I'd like to interrupt here. You all know about the research involving the feminization and masculinization of the fetal hypothalamus; we've talked about it here. It more than suggests the possibility that Miss Turner's transsexual condition is inborn. In fact, it is not only my personal belief that it is, but it is also being documented in studies by other doctors.

"We know very little about human sexuality and the perplexing physiological and psychological components of sex identity and behavior. The subject is still in its earliest stages. Only by learning about all aspects of sexual development and behavior can we understand conditions such as transsexualism, which exists as an entity, separate from transvestism and homosexuality.

"It is unfortunate, but true that the major reason for the slow progress in these areas lies in the taboos felt almost as strongly among medical scientists as among the general population. The stability of one's given sex remains untouchable—a sacred cow, if you will.

"Even among professionals like ourselves, negative moral judgments are common. But if we concentrate on the physiological and hormonal components that influence sex behavior and identity, we may be able to move beyond our own personal and emotional prejudices. If Miss Turner's life is difficult for us to understand, you can imagine how difficult it has been for her all her life."

He turned to Tina and said, "Miss Turner, thank you very much. You have been extremely helpful. We are all very appreciative."

Later, Tina realized that if men and women in medicine and other fields of science could not accept or understand what she had done and why, the rest of the world would probably be less understanding and accepting. Tina Turner was not going to have an easy time of it. That would be her challenge.

18
Journey to Freedom

The next few months were uneventful as Tina continued to recuperate from surgery. The site of the surgery remained tender, and she often experienced leg pain, especially in the left ankle where she had shot off her foot. She was tired much of the time and seldom left the house. Dr. Greenfield and her surgeon were among the very few people she saw; her appointments with them were never broken.

Following Dr. Greenfield's suggestion, Tina spent much of her time writing her life story, hoping Dr. Greenfield would use it for a book about her life. She also found writing about life events and issues to be therapeutic, and would discuss them with Dr. Greenfield at their sessions.

Tina was especially fascinated with material about transsexualism that Dr. Greenfield loaned her. She felt comforted knowing that transsexualism, homosexuality, and other gender identity disorders went back in time to Greek mythology. In therapy she learned that many present ideas they discussed dated back to Greek culture. She read about Venus Castina, a goddess who responded with sympathy and understanding to feminine souls trapped in male bodies. Tina identified with those men who wanted to be transformed into women. She learned that all this wasn't just a figment of her imagination! With great interest, she read the writings of the Roman poet, Manilius, about men who hated the very sight of themselves as men, just as she had... how these men wore robes and curled their hair. And she read about prominent historical figures of the 16th to 18th centuries, such as King Henry III, who was referred to as "Her Majesty." In 1557 King Henry III appeared in public dressed as a woman, wearing a low-cut dress and long pearl necklace. No one dared laugh or taunt him. One of the most colorful historical figures she enjoyed reading about was Francois Timoleon, also known as Abbe de Choisy and Chevalier d'Eon, who was said to be the mistress for Louis XVI and rival of Madame de Pompadour. Tina learned that the first colonial governor of New York, Lord Cornbury, was wearing a woman's dress when he arrived from England during his time in office. She thought, *These men were not ashamed of appearing as women, so why should I?*

Tina continued to see her electrologist on a regular basis. Electrolysis was a very important appointment for Tina. Any noticeable hair growth on her face created panic; it was an instant reminder of a man's beard. Electrolysis had always been painful, but now that estrogen hormones were forbidden to her, each hair seemed to have taken deeper root and grown stronger; her sessions with the electric needle were almost torture. At times she cried from pain, so Dr. Greenfield taught her self-hypnosis, which provided some relief.

Hilda Pine had been her electrologist from the beginning, and by this time they were friends. They would have coffee and chat together before a treatment. When the session concluded, Hilda applied soothing cream on Tina's face.

Hilda was from Sweden. She was attractive and had an intriguing accent that fascinated Tina. Frequently Tina invited Hilda to her home for dinner or to a movie, but Hilda always refused.

One day Tina learned that Hilda was going back to Sweden to marry her boyfriend. That news depressed Tina. She felt that she was losing her only friend. Hilda offered to sign her lease over to Tina. It was a wonderful stroke of luck. Hilda's one-bedroom apartment was larger than Tina's. It was in a nicer building, in a better neighborhood, and the rent was just a little more than she was paying for her present apartment.

One evening, Tina ventured out to explore her new neighborhood, and she came upon a nice-looking restaurant and bar a few blocks away. Deciding to splurge and have dinner out, she sat at a table facing the bar. She noticed two young women without dates flirting with some men at the bar, and a man on a bar stool who kept looking at Tina through the barroom mirror. They exchanged glances and minutes later he came over to Tina's table.

"Mind if I sit down?"

"Please do." She was flattered that he was attracted to her.

He introduced himself as Bill. He was a good-looking man with a well-trimmed small black beard. When he told her he was a traveling salesman in town for the night, they both laughed. The conversation was amiable, and eventually he asked if he could take her home. After dinner, Bill escorted Tina home, and it wasn't long after that that they were in bed.

Tina didn't know what she had expected, but she certainly did not expect intercourse to hurt. It did, and badly, but she never let him know. She expected to be excited, really aroused. After all, wasn't that what every woman was supposed to want: sex with a good-looking man? But she wasn't aroused. She paid attention to what he was doing, rather than feeling what he was doing. The sensations were not at all like what she had expected.

"You were great," he said to her, and kissed her goodbye before he left. As far as Tina could tell, he didn't know she was a transsexual.

As Tina told Dr. Greenfield about the sexual encounter,

she complained. "I didn't have an orgasm, I didn't even get aroused. What's the matter with me now? I'm a woman. I thought I was supposed to enjoy sex."

"There are any number of reasons why it wasn't what you expected. Don't forget, your surgery wasn't very long ago."

"I guess so. Maybe I was too scared he'd hurt me."

"Maybe so."

"But it really did hurt. Is it supposed to?"

"Perhaps the first couple of times," Dr. Greenfield said. "Ask your surgeon about that. He should know what you could expect."

"I'll ask Dr. Grant next time I see him." Tina added, "You know, this guy couldn't tell I wasn't born a woman."

"So your doctor was right when he said you'd fool lovers."

"And I did!" She paused, and then spoke very seriously. "He was really very good sexually. Dr. Greenfield, do you think I'll ever have a good sexual relationship with a man?"

"It's too soon to say. Don't be too hard on yourself, Tina. Just having a female body doesn't mean everything will be just the way you expected it to be."

"But I've waited so long to really be a woman . . . "

"You're just beginning to adjust to having a woman's body. You have things to learn, things to experience. Be patient."

"I guess I expected the surgery to immediately improve my sex life. Can you tell me something about a transsexual's sex life after surgery?"

"As I keep telling you, each person is a unique individual. Many male transsexuals have no sex life. They have low levels of testosterone, which normally enhances sex drive or the libido, as we sometimes call it. Your testosterone level has diminished greatly, except for that which is still secreted from your adrenal glands. You might enjoy the body closeness of your sex partner, especially if you care for the person. There may be some skin responses and breast sensations you'll enjoy when caressed. No doubt the surgeon left some nerve endings in the genital area to give you sexual pleasure, but again, your doctor is the expert on this topic."

Tina started attending classes for medical secretaries, and she was filled with enthusiasm. Highly motivated, hoping one day to work for her surgeon, she was doing very well. On a day-to-day basis it was the major event of her life. Her classmates, though much younger than she, seemed to like her. They ate lunch together, took breaks at the same time, shopped for clothes together, and generally behaved like a group of young women having a good time.

The next month, a former neighbor from her days as Timmy enrolled at the school. The neighbor recognized her immediately. Shortly after, the girls found excuses not to be with Tina. She found herself alone, avoided by almost all the women in her classes.

One day the director asked her to come to his office. Standing stiffly, with arms folded he said, "I understand you're a transsexual."

"I'm legally a woman," Tina replied.

"Don't change the subject," he snapped. "Who do you think you're fooling? Just look at you." He took her by the arm and pulled her in front of a mirror. "Do you really think you look like a woman? Your neck is too thick. Your hands and wrists are too big. And your voice sounds like a man's, not a woman's."

Tina started to cry. As she turned to leave, he said to her, "And another thing, you're not to use the ladies' room. Find somewhere else to go, but do not use the women's lavatory. Do I make myself clear?"

Tina was frustrated and despondent as she recounted the

experience at her next session with Dr. Greenfield. "I felt so humiliated. What am I going to do now? It was so nice being part of a group. It was so comfortable! Now no one there will have anything to do with me."

Dr. Greenfield spoke gently. "You may recall, I told you things like this might happen. This is the first incident. There may and probably will be others. It's tough out there. I don't think New Jersey has anti-discrimination laws specifically for those who change their gender, although transsexuals might be protected under the law. There have been some reported cases in which other transsexuals have had to use segregated bathrooms. And there was an Eastern Airlines pilot, a decorated Vietnam Vet, who flew twenty-five combat missions. He was fired when his transsexual identity became known. The Federal Civil Rights Act of 1964 attempted to protect transsexuals from discrimination, but the U.S. Circuit Court of Appeals overturned it. If you want to pursue this legally, you would have to retain a lawyer to represent you."

"I could never afford an attorney. I'll just drop out of school and go back to my welding job where I was accepted."

Tina decided to return to Montrose, Alabama before returning to her job as a welder. She called her ex-wife, Grace, who agreed to meet with her at a motel near her home.

Grace was as lovely as ever, with no noticeable change in her appearance. They greeted each other warmly, and embraced for several moments. Grace then stood back and looked at Tina, trying to deal with her ex-husband's transformation to a woman. "You look lovely," she managed to say with tears streaming down her face and emotion choking her voice. "Come with me to my house. Our children are away at camp, so I can show you their rooms and photos. My husband is attending a medical convention out West. I'm sorry you won't get to meet him."

At her next session with Dr. Greenfield, Tina told her about her visit with Grace and wept when saying how much she missed her children and Grace. However, she was relieved that they were well and happy.

"Do you think I'll ever marry, Dr. Greenfield?"

"Some transsexuals do marry after their surgery. I think it's important to be up front with your significant other that you are a transsexual before marrying; otherwise, there might not be any trust in your relationship. Your partner might feel deceived and hate you for it, and might even panic and harm you. Your partner should love and accept you as a person and for who you are despite your medical history. That does not mean you have to wear a sign and inform people who are not significant in your life that you are a transsexual."

"Now that I met with Grace, I feel up to meeting with my mother. I hope our meeting will go as well. You know my brother told me to stay away from my mother and family?"

"Let's hope for the best," Dr. Greenfield said, and then in a whisper added, "and prepare for the worst."

Feeling apprehensive, Tina delayed contacting her mother. The letter she had sent to her mother telling her what had happened went unanswered, and Dr. Greenfield warned her that the meeting, if it occurred, might be very difficult and painful. She kept postponing the call, telling herself that she would wait until she was fully recovered from her surgery. There was finally no excuse any longer. She called. Jimmy answered the phone. "Timmy?"

"No. It's Tina now."

"Yeah. Mom told us. Uh, how're you doing? Everything okay?"

"Fine. Jimmy," feeling the conversation was pointless, Tina continued, "can I speak to Mom?"

"I don't know..."

"You know what's happened . . . I've had my sex-change operation. I want Mom to see me."

"I'm not sure she'd want to see you."

"Why don't you let her decide for herself?"

"Well . . ."

"Jimmy, please. She's my mother too. A lot has happened to me. I haven't seen her for years. Can you blame me for wanting to see her now? And have her see me as a woman?"

After a pause Jimmy replied, "Okay. I'm taking Mom to a church bazaar tomorrow afternoon. It's open to the public."

"What time and where?"

"Rock Baptist Church. It's on Elm, not far . . ."

"I'll find it. What time?"

"We plan to be there at three."

"I'll find you there."

At three the next afternoon, Tina sat in her car across from the Rock Baptist Church. She was amazed at how calm she felt. At 3:20, she recognized Jimmy as he helped their mother out of the car and into the church lobby. A couple of minutes later, Tina followed and made herself inconspicuous until she saw Jimmy alone.

He hadn't changed much at all. He was balding and he had a little paunch, and he looked much as he did standing behind the counter in R.L.'s restaurant.

"Hello, Jimmy," Tina said.

Jimmy stared, taking in her changed physical appearance and the clothes she wore.

"Don't you have anything to say?"

"Yes."

"Well?"

"Why did you have to do it?" Jimmy's voice was quivering.

Tina didn't reply. Jimmy's comment fractured her composure, but she was determined to not cry.

"Look," Jimmy said. "I have to go somewhere from here. So I'll let you take Mom home . . . if she'll go with you. If not, I'm sure she can get a ride with somebody else." He left in a hurry.

Filled with anxiety, she walked over to her mother. "Hi, Mom."

Her mother turned and stared, she was speechless.

"You recognize me, don't you, Mom?"

"Well I recognize your voice . . . and I guess I'd recognize you anyhow. You don't look so bad."

For a moment they looked at each other. Janet was sixty-two now and still attractive. Over the years she maintained a trim figure, and her height remained just a bit over five feet. Her hair was still its natural color with only a few touches of gray.

"Well, I guess everyone has to live their own life," her mother said, thinking it was the nicest thing she could say.

"Would you like to join me for dinner?" Tina asked. The moment was filled with tension, and Tina wished the ground she was standing on would open up and swallow her. But she kept thinking of Dr. Greenfield's words, *Hope for the best and prepare for the worst.*

"Well . . . "

"Please, Mom."

"Well . . . all right."

After the church service they rode together in Tina's car. During the car ride to Tina's apartment her mother didn't say much, as if she were shy or uncomfortable. Tina noticed her discomfort but took the opportunity to ask questions and catch up on family details. R.L. was in a veterans' facility, very ill with a heart condition. Joe was married, had three children, and was a successful businessman. Jimmy had also married; he was a salesman, in town for a few days.

Tina parked the car in front of her building. "I thought I'd make dinner for us, Mom." Her mother nodded. Tina showed her around the apartment, pointing out her own personal touches with great pride.

"Very nice," her mother said.

"Thank you." The moment was awkward.

"You could use some new curtains in the living room," her mother said.

"I know."

"I'll make them for you if you get the material."

"You will? That would be wonderful!" That meant her mother would come back.

There was little conversation and long periods of silence during the simple meal. Tina's sex change was not discussed. She showed her mother pictures of Grace and the boys.

"Very nice."

An hour later, Tina drove her mother home.

"See you soon, Mom? About the curtains, I'll bring the material over to you."

"Yes, take care," as she got out of the car.

Tina drove home, full of conflicting feelings. The meeting had not been easy, but then, a long time had passed and much had happened. Her mother said she liked the apartment and even offered to make new curtains; that must mean she wanted to see Tina again. They hadn't argued the entire time they were together; it was probably the first real conversation she had had with her mother. Tina was encouraged that there might be hope for a relationship with her mother.

The next day Tina bought curtain material to take to her mother's apartment. For days after that, she stayed home, afraid she'd miss her mother's phone call. As time passed and she didn't hear from her mother, her hopes faded. Once, she dialed her mother's number, but she recognized Jimmy's voice and hung up.

Soon thereafter, Tina learned that her stepfather had died, and her brother didn't want her to attend the funeral. He felt that Tina would embarrass the family. A few months later, Tina took her mother to R.L.'s gravesite and planted flowers.

"I'm sorry I wasn't able to see him," Tina said to Dr. Greenfield. "I had called the nursing home often to inquire about his health and sent him a plant. I never got to talk to him, and he never knew I changed my sex. Dr. Greenfield, I really loved him, but I was never sure of his feelings toward me. When he drank he always put me down and told me I was no good."

Her mother didn't seem to care any more for Tina than she had cared for Timmy. The child-like sense of desperate disappointment and sad isolation would probably remain with her forever. The curtain material remained in its wrapper at the bottom of a closet in Tina's apartment.

19
Farewell Procrustean Bed

"I just don't like the way men behave!" Tina complained to Dr. Greenfield. Tina was furious after spending the night with a man she met at a neighborhood bar. "Men don't have any respect. They act like an octopus, always groping me! They just assume that they can do whatever they want. I don't want to be treated like that!"

"Maybe you haven't met the right kind of men," Dr. Greenfield suggested. "They're not all the same, you know. Tina, it was a pickup at a bar. He probably didn't want anything more than a one-night stand."

"What am I supposed to do? I want to be treated with respect."

"There are other ways to meet men. Find a social club to join or an organization that does things you're interested in. They're always glad to have new members, and you might have a common interest with the group."

"But what if they know me from before my change, and don't want to have anything to do with me?"

"Why don't you join a group in a different town, or even in Manhattan? Make a fresh start."

"I don't know, Dr. Greenfield. Maybe I'm not ready to socialize with men just yet. I feel so uncomfortable when they come on to me."

"Could it be that you are sexually turned off by men for the same reasons you felt hate and disgust for your male body? Perhaps having a male for a sex partner is not for you at this time."

"I don't know. I'm so confused."

At the following session, Tina was in a much better mood. "Hilda's back! She returned from Sweden and decided not to marry her boyfriend as planned. They had been apart for so long that they no longer share common interests. I'm going to see her tomorrow and resume my electrolysis treatments with her!"

"Where will she live now that you are the tenant in her former apartment?"

"She is staying with a man she had been dating here in the States. I told her she could stay with me until she found another place, but she said no."

"Are you upset that Hilda is living with a man?"

"I guess I'm jealous. I feel that she is more than a friend. Anyhow, I really would like to have a close relationship with her." Tina brushed tears from her face.

"Don't you think you should wait a while before you try to get involved in a relationship? To begin with, we have to explore your emotional and sexual feelings. In the written material you shared with me, you always had a persistent inhibition of sexual desires that you thought was due to your gender identity disorder and depression. You even might have been asexual, although there were occasions you had an orgasm fantasizing you were a woman. You never seemed to have a genuine desire to engage in sexual activity. If you want to have sex because it's pleasurable that is one thing. However, if you intend to use sex as a vehicle for socialization that's another."

"But I've waited so long to have friends... I can't stand the loneliness. What am I to do?"

Dr. Greenfield explained. "For one thing, you have to be a friend to have a friend. Friendship implies liking a person and admiring his or her personal qualities. A friend is someone you can trust. A true friend is sensitive to your emotional needs and has compassion and empathy. Friendship works best when you both have a sense of humor and an ability to share interests. Also, you mentioned before, you want to be treated with respect."

"My former wife was and is everything a friend should be, but that doesn't help me now."

Dr. Greenfield continued. "I don't know if you have ever been in love. Even when you were married to Grace you were involved with Tina. Lovers are usually preoccupied with each other and devoted to one another. They usually give the other person priority over any other relationships. As Timmy, Tina was your priority, making it difficult for you to give Grace the kind of devotion needed in romantic love. And, of course, your lack of libido was another factor. It would help for you to recognize and deal with these issues before you become involved with someone in a serious romantic relationship."

"I know what you say is right, but I'm still confused. I would like to lead a normal life and be married. I would like to be part of a family. But then I have trouble picturing myself married to a man. I am only comfortable having a close relationship with a woman," Tina said softly.

"As I said before, you need time and experience living as a woman before you become involved with anyone. It would take a magic wand to help you resolve these problems so quickly. It is going to take hard work over a period of time. Also a lot has to do with your attitude. There is a saying that life is ten percent what happens to you and ninety percent how you react to it. You have to deal with a lot of changes. Begin with short-term goals that will lead to desirable long-term consequences.

"Tina, let me sum up your concerns and share some information that might help you better understand your situation. You talk about your desire to lead a normal life. Everyone has his or her own 'normal.' What is 'normal' for one individual is not necessarily 'normal' for another."

"Dr. Greenfield, what do you mean by 'normal'?"

"Tina, everyone has a pattern of behavior, a certain manner in which they behave. It could be a reaction to people or events. For example, if you get up at the same time every morning, that's your normal, and not necessarily mine. The goal of therapy is to help the patient change from dysfunctional to functional behavior, as identified by the patient. In your case, to have a positive inner sense of self and good relationships with others are some of your goals.

"Remember that each person is a unique individual with his or her own agenda, strengths, and limitations. Each person also has the potential to change and work toward their goals, within reason. A patient has to select his or her goals, and as a therapist I'll try to help you achieve these goals. A therapist does not impose goals on a patient.

"Loneliness is a normal and common feeling experienced by transsexuals, and so is unhappiness. They often feel rejected, misunderstood, and ignored, as you do. They yearn for acceptance and understanding. They feel out of the loop. They march to the beat of a different drummer, and that confuses many people.

"As for having a so-called 'normal' marriage, you first have to confront your sex problems. It appears that you always had inhibited sexual desires. Added to that, you underwent estrogen therapy, which is known to reduce a man's sex drive to zero. The result is hormonal castration, dramatically reducing or eliminating a man's libido or sex drive. You also seem conflicted as to which sex attracts you. Most male transsexuals perceive themselves as being females and usually want a male partner. In your case, this has not been true, as you abhor intimacy with a male. So you differ from the 'normal' transsexual group, which is okay because each person is indeed a unique individual."

"Dr. Greenfield, to make matters worse I have strong feelings and attraction for my electrologist and still love my ex-wife. Does that make me lesbian, because I'm now a woman?"

"Tina, ask yourself if you will be content to have only a social life and not a sexual life as a woman with these people. You still appear to be disinterested in having a sex life with either men or women. You never wanted sex, did you? You didn't have conversion surgery as a reason to justify sexual desires but to live your life as a woman. Is that correct?"

"I guess so. Grace said she would always love me as a person . . . not as a man or a woman. I have to reprogram my thinking along those lines, as you would say. But I also keep struggling between who I was before and who I am now. I want so much to be accepted by those I know, by society, and to lead a reasonable, productive life. Who am I? Do I have a split personality?"

"That's an interesting question. It has been said that a transsexual usually has two distinct personalities but not a split personality as you referred to before. In your case, one sex identity or personality was Timmy and the other Tina. As you know, Timmy's personality is pretty much gone now, but not forgotten, and Tina's is dominant, and will likely grow, now that you had the conversion surgery. I've had many patients with multiple personalities, perhaps what you refer to as a split personality. Usually a multiple-personality individual has little or no awareness of their other personalities. For example, Timmy would not be aware that Tina existed and would probably get lost in a time period during a transition from being Timmy to becoming Tina. In your case, as Timmy, you knew Tina was there. And I don't know of any multiple-personality patients who wanted sex change surgery, despite the fact that their other personality might be of the opposite sex."

"Oh, I almost for to tell you... last week I saw a proctologist for an examination to check for cancer. He performed a digital exam and used a viewing scope. He informed me that I have hemorrhoids."

"Really?" said Dr. Greenfield.

"There's more to the story. After the exam, the proctologist's face became ashen, as he told me I was the first female he ever examined or knew who had a prostate gland."

"You never informed him that you were a transsexual?"

Tina shook her head side-to-side and smiled.

At the next session, Tina said she was unhappy because her relationship with her mother continued to be distant.

"Perhaps your mother isn't capable of being any different. Maybe her own mother was also cold and distant toward her, and consequently, she lacks the ability to have warmth and compassion as a mother."

"Maybe," Tina replied sadly. "But she is nicer to my brothers and likes their wives more than she liked mine."

"Didn't you say your brother's wife comes from a well-known family, and your brothers are successful businessmen?"

"Yes. I guess I'm just a loser and always will be in her eyes. Everyone likes a winner."

"Perhaps we should spend some time in therapy discussing the wounded child within you. We know that the neglected wounded inner child often becomes the source of an adult's human misery and not just for a transsexual. When a child feels unloved by his parents, the child sometimes grows up not knowing exactly who he is, and whether he is capable of ever being loved or accepted by others. The child often feels that if his own mother doesn't love him, who else would? The wounded inner child often contaminates his or her adult life with chronic depression and a sense of emptiness, and that emptiness usually leads to loneliness. Let's work on your inner conflicts so that the past will not trouble you so much. Let's focus on the current relationships that are real and uncontaminated by the past rejection you felt by your parents and others. And while we are on the subject of longing for your mother's love, could it be you want a woman to love you so you can receive the nurture and love that you never received from your own mother?"

"I'll have to think about that; that's a tough one," Tina replied.

A few weeks later, Dr. Greenfield noticed that Tina was quite upset when she arrived. "What's the problem, Tina?"

"Everything is fine at work. But my family is not doing well."

"Your family? I thought things were going well between you and your mother. I thought you accepted the fact that she was distant in relating to you?"

"It's not just my mother. My son, Blythe, is now twenty-one, and he's staying at my mother's apartment while studying to become an x-ray technician. He wants to work in the hospital where Grace and his stepfather are on the staff. I found out about this yesterday when I spoke to Grace. Blythe always wanted to remember me as his father, the soldier he could be proud of. Now, Grace said Blythe does not want to see me. Grace also told me that my mother has cancer and is on oxygen all the time because she's bloated with edema. That's why she hasn't seen me.

"And my brother Jimmy had open heart surgery and was told he has less than a year to live. Grace said that my father died recently and didn't want me to attend his funeral. He left all of his estate to his wife and nothing for my brothers and me. He totally disowned me in his Will."

"I'm sorry to hear that," Dr. Greenfield said. "That was unkind of your father, but he always had difficulty dealing with problems. As for your son, Blythe might benefit from therapy to help him understand about your sex change. And as for your mother and brother, Jimmy, there is a saying: 'The old must die and the young may die.'"

"But they never got to know me as Tina . . . the real me."

"What did Grace say about your son, Richard?"

"He's eighteen now and has a girlfriend, named Joanie. They plan to marry as soon as Richard completes his courses in Hotel and Restaurant Management at a college he attends. He wants to own a restaurant and be the head chef. Joanie is studying to be a nurse. They met at the hospital where Grace works.

"Grace said Richard wants me to attend his wedding. Because Joanie is studying to be a psychiatric nurse, she understands my gender identity problem and looks forward to having me as part of their family!"

Dr. Greenfield smiled, "That's wonderful!"

"But I won't go to the wedding. I don't want to be a distraction. If I went, I know my son, Blythe, would be uncomfortable, and so would my brothers, their families, and others. I'll celebrate Richard and Joanie's marriage when they come to New York City for their honeymoon.

"I don't recall if I told you that Grace is married to a psychiatrist who is on staff at the hospital where she works? His name is Lawrence Schiffer. He has been a great role model for my sons and has tried to help them understand my sexual identity problem. It just so happens that Larry is doing research in that area and is a member of a team that includes embryologists. They have been doing research involving fetal masculinzation on a section of the brain known as the hypothalamus. Grace said that the hypothalamus is inherently feminine. Unless testicular tissue secretes testosterone during a certain period of fetal development to organize that portion of the brain along masculine lines, the hypothalamus remains forever feminine. Grace and Larry both feel this biological mishap could explain why I became a transsexual. Also, problems with my male anatomy help to support this theory: my undescended testicle, no hair on my body, my body appearance, etc.

"They also told me about the 'Eve Principle.' Some embryologists reported that all human tissue is female during the early weeks of a forming fetus. If any critical problem occurs preventing masculine differentiation during this prenatal period, the fetus may have a male body but a female brain. So it is possible that Adam was really Eve at the beginning of conception!"

"I can't tell you how pleased I am that this information was shared with you. I'm certain that Dr. McArthur and Dr. Grant are informed, if you want to discuss it with them. In my work as a neuropsychologist, I also knew about it."

"I want everyone to know about it," Tina said. "Why hasn't it been shared with the public?"

Tina brought a lot of literature to the following session. "I went to a Manhattan night spot over the weekend. It was a large restaurant and dance club that had entertainment. I was hoping to meet transsexuals like myself, who were also lonely and wanted to just have a friendly, no-sex relationship."

"Did you?"

"I met a lot of different people, but no one I felt I could be friends with. Someone told me about a symposium on Gender Dysphoria that was going to be held in Manhattan, and I attended the next day. I took a lot of notes and thought you could answer some of the questions about their presentations?"

"Tell me about it."

Tina opened her notebook. "They covered many topics.

One doctor said everyone is 'intersexed' anatomically as well as endocrinologically. That anatomical sex is not exclusively male or female; for example, nipples exist in both male and female breasts and are considered secondary sexual characteristics. And women have a rudimentary penis called a clitoris." Tina paused to spell "clitoris." "As for endocrine sex, that is also mixed in both sexes. In the male, the testes and adrenals produce small amounts of the female hormone, estrogen, as well as androgen, the male hormone. Androgen, the male hormone, can also be found in the ovaries and in larger amounts in the adrenal glands of women. The speaker went on to say that the male can become more feminized by taking estrogen and the female more masculinized by taking testosterone. Of course, I already found that out.

"Then someone spoke about Hermaphroditus, who was the son of Hermes and Aphrodite. He was so beautiful that a nymph asked the gods to merge her body with his forever, and she became half-man and half-woman. I could identify with that. I felt like I was part man and part woman, but not by choice.

"Some babies are born with ambiguous external genitalia," Tina continued, reading and spelling out some of the words as she went along. "Nursery sex mistakes sometimes occur at the time of birth in recording a baby's sex because of deformities of the sex organs, and so the legal sex is incorrectly recorded. So-called nursery sex people have organized themselves as an advocacy group and prefer to be known by the word intersex rather than hermaphrodites, or nursery sex mistakes. They publish a newsletter I read. Like me, they usually become alienated from their families and resent the way they have been treated, as if they were freaks. Some of these people were born with both ovaries and testes and sometimes with organs that look like a small penis or a large clitoris. They say that they are heterosexual in the true sense of the word. They resent entertainers displaying them as 'The Bearded Lady,' and worse.

"Then a doctor discussed how during the first six weeks of development in the womb, all embryos are sexually identical, but sometimes there is a genetic mix-up in the genetic code."

"It seems like having attended school to become a medical secretary has been put to good use." Dr. Greenfield was quite impressed with Tina's investigation of the gender identity problem.

Tina smiled and continued. "Would you believe there is a chromosomal deviation that has my last name? It's called Turner's Syndrome. That's when one of the X chromosomes is missing for a girl. The girl has forty-five instead of forty-six chromosomes, including just one X chromosome.

"In a case that relates to me, they discussed the most common defect in testicular development. As you know, I had an undescended testicle. They said an undescended testicle can be a sign of other internal sexual deviations or that the organ itself is imperfect.

"They spoke about Alan Turing. At first I thought his last name was Turner. He was one of Great Britain's most brilliant mathematicians, a code analyst, and computer pioneer. During World War II he developed the machine that broke "Enigma," Germany's most secret and complex code. His research and contributions provided the Allies with advanced information on German battle plans, which helped win the war. Instead of giving him a hero's medal, they arrested him for being guilty of 'gross indecency' because he was a homosexual. He could not tolerate the punishment imposed on him and committed suicide by eating an apple laced with cyanide. He is regarded as one of the fathers of computer science! They also mentioned other good citizens and famous homosexuals, and how society treated them badly.

"Dr. Greenfield, I'm in no way a genius like Turing, but I also served my country, was awarded five medals, and sustained injuries that almost caused me to die on the operating table. And then I got a dishonorable discharge for dressing like Tina at a bar outside the base. I was falsely accused of stealing money. I never had legal representation to defend me, and that should have been provided to me by the army."

"Was anything else discussed about chromosomes?"

Tina returned to her notebook. "They talked about some women having the Triple-X Syndrome, and Klinefelter's (XXY) Syndrome, which causes some men to have small genitals and to be sterile. And then there is the XYY Syndrome resulting in some men having delinquent, criminal, or even terrorist behavior. These people are dangerous and have to be dealt with if they hurt others."

Tina continued, "At the symposium, the topic of marriage for homosexuals and others with gender identity problems came up. They discussed a situation where a woman and a transsexual, who was born a man and had conversion surgery to become a woman, married. Even though they were considered a same sex couple, their marriage was legal because the transsexual had male chromosomes. They think same sex couples should be permitted to marry."

"Same sex marriages did occur in America," Dr. Greenfield stated. "An American Indian tribe sometimes permitted a male member to dress as a female and marry another male. Some of my homosexual patients say that they want to be able to legally marry their homosexual partner."

"Do you think this will ever happen?"

"Time will tell. Many homosexuals meet and live together as if they have a domestic or married partnership. It's harder and harder to defend the institution of traditional marriage with its soaring divorce rates, children being born out of wedlock, and pregnancy being flaunted by unmarried celebrities. There are many single mothers and fathers and many unhappy heterosexual marriages. It would be unprofessional for me to pass judgment or take sides because I have both heterosexual and homosexual patients. Eventually the issue will have to be dealt with.

"Homosexuality and sex gender disorders occur in every walk of life. It doesn't matter if the individual is a politician, lawyer, doctor, member of the clergy, actor or entertainer, or plain everyday folk. Someone would have to walk a mile in their shoes before they could begin to judge them other than just being Americans. Americans that society places on the proverbial Procrustean Bed."

"What is this Procrustean Bed you refer to?"

"There is a tale in classical Greek mythology about a robber named Procrustes who lived near Eleusis in Attica. He would kidnap travelers and place them on an iron bed in his abode. To make them conform to the length of the iron bed, he would either amputate their limbs, if they were too long, or stretch the limbs of those he captured, if they were too short.

"It has been said that the theory of non-injurious human behavior should be formulated to meet the uniqueness of the individual's needs rather than to tailor the person to fit society's Procrustean Bed."

20
Tina: An American Transsexual

"I'm back at my welding job," Tina proudly announced at the next session with Dr. Greenfield. "My boss was happy to have me back. He said I'm the best welder he ever had."

"Great! How did the others treat you?"

"All the employees in the area where I work are men. Each one said they were glad I was back, as though the boss told them to say that. They really don't bother with me and leave me pretty much to myself while I'm working, which is okay with me. The girls in the accounting and billing office are really nice to me. They invite me to join them when they go for lunch at the diner."

"What are their names?"

"Well, there's Stella. She's young enough to be my daughter, about thirty-five years old. She has short, wavy, ash-blonde hair, blue eyes, and a small turned-up nose. She's on the quiet side, very pretty, and has a lovely smile."

"Is she married?"

"Her husband and only child were killed in an auto accident two years ago. She tries to be very brave about it, but I can feel her pain. In many ways we are on the same wavelength, trying to cope in the face of devastating events in our lives. It is as if she can feel my pain too.

"Then there's Marilyn, the office manager. She's an attractive brunette, well dressed, and vivacious. She enjoys chatting and meeting new people. She's about the same height as Stella. I think she's divorced. Then there's Tammy and Jo. They are younger than me and very friendly."

"You seem to be comfortable in your setting. That's really great."

"You know, Dr. Greenfield, as Timmy, I was a very unhappy person and tried to hide my feelings from everyone. I had no friends. I never felt close to anyone and always wished I could just have one true friend. Even though I was married, and Grace was such a fine person, I felt uncomfortable and alone because I had to act masculine. I tried my best to overcome it for the sake of Grace and myself but nothing worked. I bought five suits thinking that if I got all dressed up as a man I'd feel good. You know the expression, 'Clothes make the man.' It didn't help. I still was Timmy, and I couldn't get close to anyone. Instead I got nervous, anxious, and irritable. I just wanted to be alone so I could change my clothes and be Tina. Then I became a different person. After being Tina for a while, I was nicer to my wife and children. I can't begin to tell you the agony I went through at those times, until I changed to Tina."

"Tina, I realize how difficult life was as Timmy, but it would be hard for most people to understand. There have been science fiction movies about outer space aliens who invaded earthlings' bodies, and about the inner turmoil experienced by those whose bodies were taken over. The cinema has portrayed the suffering of other characters being transformed like a Dr. Jekyll and Mr. Hyde, or a scientist turning into the Hulk, or people possessed by Satan that had to be exorcised. But in your case, Tina is a serene, good person, who needed to emerge so she could have a productive and satisfying life."

Tina nodded. "That's true. But society takes the position that a transsexual male like me only wants to be surgically altered to become a woman so he will be less lonely or for sex.

That's not the case. I needed surgery because my soul and mind could not accept my body. My body had to be surgically reshaped to conform to my soul and mind."

Most of Tina's following sessions centered on her involvement with the "girls" at work, especially Stella. Stella had invited her over for dinner. Tina loved Stella's home. It was a lovely two-family home in Mahwah, New Jersey. Stella's husband had a substantial life insurance policy, which allowed her to pay off the mortgage after his death. The upstairs tenant, Kay, was a forty-year-old woman raising a ten-year-old daughter, Carol. Kay was physically challenged resulting from multiple sclerosis that began shortly after her daughter's birth. Her husband left because he could not deal with her disability, but by court order he financially subsidized his child and wife. The rent payments helped Stella pay the taxes on her home. Stella shopped for her tenant and helped to care for her as much as possible after coming home from work. Tina also became involved helping Kay and Carol. Like Stella, Tina would shop, cook, and look after them as much as possible.

The other "girls" in the accounting department also did volunteer work. Marilyn belonged to an organization that collected clothing and food for needy Bergen Country residents. Tammy loved animals and volunteered hours at the Bergen County Animal Shelter, where she fed and walked the impounded dogs that waited to be adopted. Jo was involved with church-based charity activities and helped care for aged and infirmed parishioners.

"They are such fine people," Tina said. "I'm so lucky to be accepted by them."

"Do the girls know you are a transsexual?"

"Yes. I felt comfortable telling them about my life. Stella wept as she heard how badly my family treated me as a child. All the girls were upset that people like me and others are so mistreated. They are such good people."

"Do you plan to join any of their volunteer groups?"

"Well I do help Kay, the woman with multiple sclerosis. I would like to spend some time at the animal shelter where Tammy volunteers. The suffering these animals experience makes me wonder how people can be so cruel and indifferent to living creatures. Remember Rex, the dog who stayed by my side during those terrible days I spent on the farm? I will never forget Rex. He was the one and only friend I had as a child."

Dr. Greenfield nodded.

"I wish I could adopt one of the dogs at the shelter, but I'm not allowed to have pets in my apartment. Stella likes dogs, she has a golden retriever named Jade."

"Stella really sounds like a wonderful person and friend."

"My lease will expire next month, and Stella asked if I would like to rent the addition to her home that her father had built and lived in until he moved to the Jersey Shore. I wanted to talk to you about that."

"That sounds like a good idea."

"I'll put some of my furniture in storage just in case Stella marries, and I have to move out. Stella reminds me so much of how I imagine my daughter, Noelle, would be. I hope someday, somehow, Noelle will know I never deserted her and that her mother took her away from me so I could never see her. It would have been nice for her to know her half-brothers. Stella said I could take care of her garden. I always wanted to have a garden filled with beautiful flowers and vegetables."

"Have you met Stella's family?"

"Yes, and they have been so good to me. They include me in their family events at their shore house. I have a standing invitation to be with them for Thanksgiving and Christmas. Can you believe I am no longer alone on the holidays? They even celebrate my birthday! Stella also said I could adopt a dog from the shelter. If I do, I'll call it Rex!"

At a later session, Tina brought a newsletter from the factory where she worked. Tina was featured in a front-page photo and article titled, "A Creative and Artful Skill." Appearing with Tina in the photo were dozens of replicas of the equipment her company sold that were handcrafted by Tina. The stainless steel miniature models of the machinery were described as not only "eye-catching," but also valuable as sales aids used by the sales force to demonstrate various features and functions to prospective customers. The article reported that those who had seen Tina's models always expressed high regard for the craftsmanship and intricate detail, and that the company placed Tina's replicas on exhibition at trade shows in the U.S. and abroad. The salespeople relied heavily on the miniature models to enhance sales presentations. The only problem, the article said, was that sales reps and customers wanted to keep the replicas.

"Tina, I'm so proud of you! Your artistic work really is magnificent! Over the years, you have given me beautiful replicas of ships and airplanes you built and paintings you created. I have placed them in my office suite and on the walls. I wish you could hear the compliments people make about your work. You really are gifted."

"It gave me special pleasure making them for you and having them fit in with your décor."

The following month, Tina showed Dr. Greenfield newspaper and magazine articles her friends shared with her when they were out for their monthly dinner. "They asked me to share this information with you. There are millions of men and women undergoing extensive surgical makeovers that are both invasive and cosmetic. Some of these surgical makeovers can cause a variety of problems, infections, and even death.

One article discussed a woman who had every part of her body reshaped from head to toe. Why is it that no one objects to these procedures, but just about everyone objects to sex conversion surgery, which is essential for a transsexual's mental health? Does that make any sense to you? And here is an article about people piercing their body parts and otherwise mutilating themselves, which is considered an 'in thing' to do. But for transsexuals, who want surgery to survive, it is treated as if it is a horrible crime."

"Tina, breaking a taboo, such as sex conversion operations, always generates quick and usually negative emotions. However, as some scientists have written, the forces of nature know nothing of this taboo. The facts cannot be disputed. People who have intersex and sexual identity disorders exist, in body as well as mind. The terms 'male' and 'female' seem definite, and yet as we have covered in our sessions, it is apparent that the more sex is studied in its nature and implications, the more it loses its nature and implications. As we have discussed and you have witnessed with your own eyes, some people are born with the wrong body by accident, and they are forced to live with that body, unless of course they are Siamese twins. Then it is acceptable to correct the wrong with surgery. Other individuals with a sexual identity dysfunction that are denied help often lead two separate and secret lives, attempt or commit suicide, or even mutilate their sex organs. Still others become mentally ill because they are trapped and can't get help. We need more scientists who are guided by a patient's inherent best interest rather than to place everyone on society's Procrustean Bed.

"Tina, your courage and determination to focus attention on this matter is admirable. We are not talking about criminals. We are talking about law-abiding people being unique and entitled to enjoy peace of mind and respect."

As weeks passed, Tina's mood remained high. She

enjoyed her friends, her job, living at Stella's home, and having phone contact with her son, Richard. However, Dr. Greenfield noticed that Tina appeared to be losing weight and complained about feeling unusually tired.

"I can't tell you how much I regret shooting off my foot." Tina leaned over to rub her badly-swollen ankle where the prosthesis was attached. "It's become swollen and painful, making it harder for me to climb stairs and lead an active life with my new friends. I really thought that by shooting off my toe I wouldn't be able to wear high-heel shoes, and that I would be forced to accept my male role. I must have been terribly desperate at that point of my life, and stupid. If only I had known you back then."

"How is your health otherwise? How do you feel physically?"

"I try to keep my diabetes under control, but at times I have a problem with my vision, and that frightens me because I need good vision to do my job at work. My doctor told me that diabetes mellitus tends to run in families. My father had a severe case of diabetes at the time of his death." Then with a smirk she continued. "Well, I guess I can't say I didn't inherit anything from him. And as you know, I take medication for high blood pressure, have staples in my heart, and a continuing heart condition."

Her sessions with Dr. Greenfield continued to be interesting and productive. Tina still wrote about events in her life and gave the material to Dr. Greenfield hoping they might be useful if Dr. Greenfield decided to write a book about her life.

One day late in the year, Tina phoned Dr. Greenfield. "I just returned home from an appointment with Dr. Grant. My blood pressure was 190 over 115. I have pains in my chest and down through my left arm, and I can barely breathe. I also feel dizzy, nauseous, and sweaty."

"Call 911 and Stella immediately!"

Tina was crying. "Dr. Greenfield, I'm afraid I'm going to die!"

"Tina, they'll be able to help at the hospital. You won't die. Please call 911. Tell them you need an ambulance. Go ahead, Tina. Don't wait."

Tina was taken to the hospital by the Mahwah Volunteer Ambulance Corps and admitted to the intensive care unit. She was diagnosed with thrombophlebitis in the left leg and an embolism in her lung.

As soon as Tina was permitted to see visitors, Dr. Greenfield went to see her. Tina laid in bed, pale and thinner, looking smaller than ever. She smiled weakly at the sight of Dr. Greenfield.

"How are you feeling, Tina?"

"Very, very tired."

"I'm sure you do, but you are on the mend. You'll feel better soon."

"Did you know I almost died?"

Dr. Greenfield nodded. "Stella told me."

Tina grasped Dr. Greenfield's hand. "I want to live. I've waited so long to be a real woman. Things are going well for me now." Her eyes brimmed with tears. "Everything will be okay for me won't it, Dr. Greenfield? It's almost the end of the year, and my horoscope says that next year is going to be a good one for me."

"It's important that you have a positive attitude. It will help your recovery. I have to leave now, but I will stay in touch with you."

"Dr. Greenfield, I have an envelope for you that I took with me when I was waiting for the ambulance. It's in the drawer next to my bed." Dr. Greenfield found the envelope with her name on it, along with the words in bold lettering: "Private—to be opened in case of emergency."

"Please don't open it until you get home," Tina said with

a smile as Dr. Greenfield was leaving.

Back at her office, Dr. Greenfield found it difficult to concentrate on her work. She slowly opened the envelope Tina gave her and read the note:

Dear Dr. Natalee:
    I am writing to thank you, and to tell you how special you are to me. You and your husband are part of my life. You have always been there for me when I needed you. When I think about you, I realize that you are the friend I always prayed to have. You're there with words I need to hear, and you're always there with your understanding. You are more special to me than you could ever know. Here is a poem I wanted to share with you.

> God made me two
> Then made me one
> God made me blue
> But his work wasn't done
> He made me happy
> When he made me one.

> Love
> Tina

Dr. Greenfield took a deep breath and tried to fight back the tears. She thought about Tina's life, a life filled with struggle, pain, courage, and personal revolution. It needed to be told for Tina's sake, and for the sake of others like her. Dr. Greenfield took a pad of paper and, with pen in hand, wrote: "Listen, you've got to help me . . . I'm a transsexual."